Van Buren

OUR FREE MINDS

*Books by H. A. Overstreet*


OUR FREE MINDS

ABOUT OURSELVES

INFLUENCING HUMAN BEHAVIOR

THE ENDURING QUEST

WE MOVE IN NEW DIRECTIONS

A DECLARATION OF INTERDEPENDENCE

A GUIDE TO CIVILIZED LEISURE

# OUR FREE MINDS

*By H. A. OVERSTREET*

*

*New York*
W · W · NORTON & COMPANY · INC ·
*Publishers*

70 Fifth Avenue, New York, N. Y.

*First Edition*

PRINTED IN THE UNITED STATES OF AMERICA
FOR THE PUBLISHERS BY THE VAIL-BALLOU PRESS

# CONTENTS

## *Part Three. New Skills to Learn*



## *Part Four. New Values to Create*

# ACKNOWLEDGMENTS

I WISH to thank the Town Hall, Inc. and the Columbia University Press for the privilege of reprinting, in revised form, an address given at the Town Meeting of the Air on December 12, 1940. This revised version of the address is found in Chapters I and II. I wish also to thank the American Association for Adult Education for permission to reprint an article from the *Journal of Adult Education*, January, 1938, entitled "When Words Go Forth to Battle." The material is found in Chapter XIV.

# FOREWORD

THERE ARE two jobs which we of the present generation will have to undertake:

> one is to help defeat the new forces of barbarism that are threatening such civilization as we have achieved;
> the other is to find our American way of carrying through the economic, political, and social revolution that is sweeping the world.

These two jobs are different, but related. Neither can be completed without the other. Together they require a reshaping of our attitudes and a new discipline of our wills.

The first has in it more of terror; but the second is the more difficult. The first requires that we take the risk of being involved in the most terrible war the human race has ever experienced. The second requires that we wrench ourselves free of the familiar outlooks of the age into which we were born and shape new outlooks for the age into which we are to live. The first is but a means to the second. Unless the rule of force is successfully challenged, we simply will not have the chance to go ahead with the long job of shaping a decent human society. On the other hand, unless we are determined to shape a better society than any we have ever known, a triumph over dictatorship becomes an empty triumph—one that will, in time, breed new dictatorship and new barbarism.

Both these jobs necessitate, first of all, a clear understanding of values that are worth keeping and defending. Following this, they require an understanding of new values we shall have to put into effect.

This book has to do with clarifying our minds and disciplining our wills for the work ahead of us.

# PART ONE
# OLD VALUES TO KEEP

## ★ *I* ★

# WHAT ARE WE PREPARING TO DEFEND?

A STRONG defense of our country requires a strong conviction that our country is worth defending. Of late years there has been a growing cynicism among us about our own land, a growing disillusion about its pretensions of life, liberty, and justice for all. "America is promises," wrote Archibald MacLeish a little while ago. But to many victims of our haphazard system, America has seemed chiefly broken promises.

What is the America we are preparing to defend? Is the America we know worth defending? Are we to give it up for something supposedly better; or are we to defend it because we believe it to be profoundly good? Are we to defend it only as it is today; or also as it may become tomorrow?

## I

One of the boldest statements in all history is our American declaration that all men are created equal. It was laughed at in its day. It has been laughed at since. But in spite of its apparent absurdity, it was then and still remains the fundamental expression of our American way of life.

The statement expressed not merely a fact but an intention. Since all men were created equal in the right to fulfill their lives, we intended, then and thereafter, to build the kind of nation in which this right could be realized.

This was and remains our American credo and our American pledge. And this, more than anything else, is why America has been called a "haven"—a haven of the oppressed of all lands. America has believed in people—in all people; has believed in their basic right to be allowed to be what they have it in them to be.

Today powerful forces are challenging this belief. Hitler and his followers are proclaiming a new credo, a bitter and determined assertion of the inequality of men. They talk of a master-nation and servant-nations, of a noble Aryan race and a despised Jewish race, of privileged individuals who are of the "elite" and of underprivileged individuals who belong to the unconsidered masses. The "new order," so-called, which they seek to build is not to be a "haven" for the oppressed. It is to be itself an oppressor—of all those who, because of a wrong drop of blood or because of ideas that are forbidden, or because they oppose the rule of gangsters, are denied the dignities and rewards of life.

Herein lies the deepest conflict of our time. It is a war to the death between two ways of life: the way of generosity, compassion, co-operation, and peaceful growth; and the way of arrogance, cruelty, pitiless domination, and violent overturn.

If we have anything in America that is worth defending, it is this belief of ours in the equality of human rights. There are indeed glaring inequalities among us. We know this and are not proud of it. But to be an American means to *intend* to remove these inequalities. It means to *intend* to build a land where all have equal right to life, liberty, and the pursuit of happiness.

But the Hitler way of life is more than an arrogant assertion of inequality. It is a calculated technique for making and keeping people unequal. The technique is first and foremost the compulsory removal of all the basic freedoms: freedom of thought and speech, of assembly, of the vote, of the press, of religion, of occupation, of honest research. The only freedom remaining, it would seem, is to torture helpless people—and even this is not free; it is commanded.

People, however, do not voluntarily and happily give up their freedom; nor do decent people voluntarily and happily torture their neighbors. They have to be lied to in order to be made to do it. This is the second of Hitler's techniques. He persuades people by manufactured evidence to believe that obedience is better than freedom, that to be cruel in his special cause is nobler than to be kind. The chief instrument of this enslaving way of life is not truth–for truth sets people free; it is the "dynamic lie." For the first time in history a whole order of life is being deliberately based on lies.

Finally, the Hitler technique denies what we of the democracies believe in–that nations must peacefully grow from good to better, from better to still better. The Hitler way ruthlessly tears down and arbitrarily builds up, and then proudly proclaims that this jerry-built structure of life will "last a thousand years."

## II

What we have to defend in America is the opposite of all this. We have first of all to defend our right to *grow*–peacefully–by trial and error, by observation and fumbling, by learning now this and now that. We have to defend ourselves against fixation by command. But in order to grow, we have to be free–to think and to discuss, to say "No" on our ballots if we mean "No." We have to be free in our worship, free in our choice of occupation. Our press must be free; teachers and scientific researchers must be free in their service of truth. If these freedoms go, everything goes; for only out of the full liberty of the spirit can wisdom and justice increase among us.

There is something utterly basic about this right to be free. All life, all government has to change. There are, however, two ways of change: the way of violence and the way of reason. Violence accomplishes change swiftly and dramatically; but it accomplishes it by doing violence to *people*—to human nature itself. It gives people no time for the slow processes of growth. It makes them over by command. But a whole people cannot be made over by command. Change, to be genuine, must be a change wrought in their minds, hearts, and habits. Only the free way of reason can bring about such deeper change. This is the way of democracy. Freedom to think and discuss, to fumble and fail and try again; freedom to know why we are doing what we are asked to do—this is the freedom necessary if changes are to be wrought truly and lastingly in the minds, hearts, and habits of people.

These rights—of human equality, freedom, and peaceful growth—we are prepared to defend, because basic to our democratic view of life is respect for human beings. There are those who will laugh at this, who will point out the many forms of ugly disrespect for human beings and of downright oppression of them in our present America. There are those who will remind us that we have among us individuals who care more about property rights than human rights; who would sell democracy down the river if thereby they could make their privileges and profits more secure.

This is true. There is an enemy that lurks in our midst. It is the same enemy that sold out France and almost sold out Britain. We have that enemy in America—privileged people who fear labor more than they fear Hitler; who fear social legislation more than they fear the power of fascism.

But perhaps, also, we have an enemy far more widely among us than we are in the habit of recognizing. This enemy is our private intolerances; our muddleheadednesses; our narrow preoccupation with our private advantage; our social snobbishnesses and hatreds; our readiness to go witch-hunting; our persecution of people we do not like; our easy surrender to slogans and isms. One hundred and thirty million people *can* be wrong. All too easily we draw a black-white picture of America—an angel-devil picture. We like to talk of the few exploiters—the people of swollen wealth—and the many virtuous exploited ones. This gives us, the virtuous ones, a sense of self-pity and self-esteem. But it is probably true that most Americans would like to be immensely rich if they could possibly make the grade; to that end, they would not be averse to exploiting their fellows right royally if they had the chance. Also, it is not only a few rich people who call the Negro a "nigger"; or who crab at relief to the unemployed; or who cry out against paying union wages; or who break up meetings; or who fire liberal-minded teachers. It is average men and women of the average towns and homes of America who do these things. And it is these things that are a chief enemy of our democracy.

If we are going to defend America, we shall have to remember that it must be *we* who must do the defending. Do we—the average people of America—show by our attitudes and practices that we believe in the democracy we are preparing to defend? For example, do we believe in it enough to pay higher taxes for more playgrounds, for better schools and libraries, for better housing and city planning? These are all necessary for a high-grade democracy; and they cost money. Do we believe in democracy enough to devote the energies of our minds to discovering how to correct inequalities and injustices in our midst? "Eternal vigilance is the price of liberty." Translated into peace terms, this means a continuous, day-by-day alertness to conditions that threaten the common welfare. Translated into local terms, it means a willingness to ferret out scandalous conditions in our neighborhoods and communities. If we are merely a people uttering pious platitudes about democracy while in private life we practice either the arts of antidemocracy or the art of civic somnolence, America will be but poorly defended.

Because—thanks to our forefathers—life has gone along fairly happily for many of us in America, we have become slack in our democratic faith. We have held it as we hold our religion—good for special occasions. In this time of crisis, when a new and powerful barbarism is preparing to beat down our defenses, our first obligation must be a rethinking of what we ourselves, as average Americans, believe about democracy and are willing to do about it and for it. If it really means to us liberty, equality, and justice for all, we have to do what we can to make these come alive in the spot where we stand.

If we are planning to defend the democratic way of life, we ourselves will have to be democratic enough in spirit and practice to be its rightful defenders.

★ 2 ★

# GETTING DOWN TO PARTICULARS

## I

LET us ask ourselves, clearly and strongly, what we are *not* preparing to defend.

We are not preparing to defend racial discrimination in any of its forms. By this we mean anti-Semitism. By this we mean the denial to the Negro of the full rights of a human being. And we mean it particularly at a time when Jim Crowism is threatening to become the law of the army. The Negro soldier must be treated as a full American citizen and not as a segregated pariah. How can we, without utter contempt for our own hypocrisy, ask any human being to defend a country that treats him with contempt?

We are not preparing to defend the cowardly methods of the Ku Kluxers, Silver Shirts, Black Eagles, or any other self-constituted group of snoopers, persecutors, and extralegal lawmakers. We are not preparing to defend lynching—in the North, East, South, or West. We are not preparing to defend poll-tax slavery.

We are not preparing to defend the right of corrupt political machines to own our cities, nor the right of state and national machines to grow strong through the spoils system.

We are not preparing to defend the denial to any American citizen of his civil liberties, even though the denial be made in the name of a national emergency.

We are not preparing to defend governmental favors to powerful violators of the labor act. We do not remember that industry has offered, for patriotic reasons, to take a loss. We do not see that labor should be compelled to do what industry has refused to do. We are not preparing to defend labor racketeering. We are not preparing to defend poverty in the midst of plenty. We are not preparing to defend the enormous and irresponsible power exercised by the great owners of wealth. We are not preparing to defend any form of free enterprise that is a pious cloak for exploitation.

These things we are *not* preparing to defend. Moreover, these things we are not preparing to condone. They are, one and all, a disgrace to America. We are a democracy. We intend to defend what is democratic. We cannot be half-democratic and half-antidemocratic and hope to be a strong people.

A strong defense requires a strong conviction. We

cannot have a strong conviction if we compromise the values in which we believe.

## II

Our democratic way of life, we have said, is a way of respect for all human beings. This respect calls for more than verbal acceptance. To defend democracy we must act out democracy.

At this time of crisis, what are the ways in which we can act out democracy?

A first way is to practice freedom of discussion. It is to listen to what the other fellow has to say, even though what he has to say is to us anathema. Without free and generous discussion democracy is dead.

A second way is to extend and enrich all the educational opportunities of our people, from infancy through adulthood. To curtail education in the name of defense would be to weaken that very defense. A powerful people must be an enlightened people.

A third way is to increase among us all the possible forms of voluntary co-operation. Democracy is a way of associating people together for their common welfare. Every consumers' co-operative puts into practice this voluntary, associated way of life. So does every credit union. So does every form of group medicine. So does every form of co-operative housing. The more effectively Americans learn to work together for a common good the more truly are they democratic in practice.

A fourth way is by the further expansion of the method of insurance. Insurance is a pooling of the resources of all for the protection of each. It is the most effective and self-respecting way we know of meeting the disasters of unemployment and the diminished earning power of old age. Social insurance is democracy intelligently in action.

A fifth way is to make our care for those in distress increasingly considerate. This holds for the Community Chest, for the Red Cross, for every community hospital. It also holds for a willing, generous, and non-pauperizing form of relief for our unemployed.

A sixth way is to do justice to the worker. For a long enough time, the worker has been the chattel slave of business, industry, and finance. We make our democracy come alive when we give the worker the chance to stand equal with the employer. Those who oppose or evade or violate collective bargaining, in letter or in spirit, are foes of democracy.

A seventh way is for the worker, in his millionfold power, to do justice to himself, to his employer, and to the public. A racketeering union that has become not a service agency for the rights of labor, but a gangster agency that gyps labor, employer, and public alike, has no place in a democracy. Such unions set us back rather than forward, for they break our faith in a necessary democratic tool.

Finally, there is an eighth way. Perhaps it is the most important of all. We began as a nation of communities. As we have grown in numbers and complexity, our communities, in the fine old sense, have almost vanished. We are a nation of people who do not know one another and who have too largely lost the art of thinking and working together. What we basically need in America is to recover the strength and the spirit of the community. The best defense of America will come not from the top down but from the bottom up—from the thousands of communities that are coming alive to their common needs and their common problems.

But these eight ways of acting out democracy are not yet enough. We shall not fulfill our democratic aims until we have contrived, somehow, by some means, to guarantee to every American a decent living wage. Millions of Americans are without such a wage. They are the victims of undernourishment, miserable housing, and lifelong insecurity. We have begun to see our obligation to the unemployed; we shall some day see our obligation to the marginal worker.

Again, we shall not fulfill our democratic aims until we have learned somehow, by some means, to let the rich abundance of our land flow into the lives of all our people. An economic system that halts that flow, that diverts it into the control of a few, is an economic system that democracy must drastically overhaul.

We have a great tradition to defend. It is the tradition of a free people freely dedicated to the achievement of liberty and justice for all. It is this conception of a free people, freely dedicated to the achievement of liberty and justice for all, that the whole totalitarian system despises and denies. It glorifies the god-man, who says the saving word. To us, this god-man seems far more like a monster, who says the enslaving word. It glorifies submission to the state. We believe in the consent of the governed. It glorifies the power of the lie. We believe in the freedom of truth. It glorifies violence. We believe in the ways of peace. It glorifies the oppression of the weak by the strong. In our civilization, even children scorn the bully. They say, "Pick on somebody your own size!" In the totalitarian states it has become a virtual command to pick on somebody—individual or small nation—that you are sure you can terrorize with impunity.

It is against all this utter perversion of life that democracy is prepared to defend itself. We are far from perfect. We fumble and fail; we commit injustice; we are cruel to our own people. But basically the original intention still holds—to build a land where liberty, equality, and justice can be for all. We are prepared to defend our right to carry out this intention.

# ⋆ 3 ⋆

# WEAK PLACES IN OUR DEFENSE

## I

An acid of doubt, we have said, has eaten into many of our people. They are not so sure that democracy is the great way of life it has been made out to be. After the last World War, they were disillusioned about its power to save the world. After eleven years of economic depression, they have begun to doubt its power even to save itself. They see millions of people still out of work, a national budget still unbalanced, taxes mounting, banks filled with money no one is able to employ; they hear charges of corruption and inefficiency. Meanwhile the politicians talk. They seem always to be talking. They seem never to be doing anything that approaches a solution of our problems.

It should not be surprising if such people were to lend an uneasy ear to the European taunt that government by talk can never be government that succeeds. Ours, unfortunately, has been government by a huge amount of talk. Unfortunately, too, for the most part, it has been talk by men untrained in governmental knowledge and wisdom. When many men who know little talk much, can much be expected? Even the average American, who himself may not know much, has a half-humorous, half-angry contempt for the men whom he periodically invests with the power to govern. He has contempt; but even he is helpless to think how, under a democratic process, a wiser choice of men might be made; even he is helpless to think how those who govern him might be educated for the art of governing. He merely takes it for granted that democratic politics are and will continue to be a mess.

Nor would it be so bad if political talk were always honest talk. The average citizen knows there are indeed honest men in government; but at the same time he remembers the shame of our cities, the scandals of Tammany Hall, of the Prendergast ring, of one notorious poker-playing federal administration. He knows about Hague in Jersey City, and the Kelly-Nash machine in Chicago.

So he is not altogether unready to believe that there are serious, perhaps fatal, weaknesses in democracy. Now that Hitler has surprised the world with his amazing power to weld a whole nation into dynamic unity, many Americans are prepared to have doubts about our own democratic superiority. Before the terror of recent events, one heard Americans saying: "Yes, Hitler's pretty bad, but . . ." The "but" always meant that here was a man who could brush aside bureaucratic red tape, governmental palaver, the endless procrastinations of politicians, and snap things into action.

Americans, in short, have been having doubts about the way we do things. It is probably true that if our land should be attacked, the doubts would vanish in a concerted effort to save ourselves. It would be better, however, if we could get at the doubts now. What *is* the matter with America? Can we honestly face our weaknesses? Can we tell ourselves just how ignorant and inefficient we are? Or, if danger comes, will we repeat the old patriotic hokum—waving the flag and jailing every honest citizen who asks us to think about our own shortcomings?

*Our first line of defense will have to be a dead honesty with ourselves.*

We shall have to prove to ourselves that we have the stuff in us that can stand criticism of ourselves. France needed that stuff and did not have it. England seems to have it. Between now and the time when we ourselves may have to fight for our lives, we shall need to become honest about our democratic way of life.

We can already hear ardent patriots shouting: "This is no time for criticism." These hasty patriots are among the enemies of America. In a democracy, as in the case of an individual, Socrates' wisdom still holds: "An unexamined life is not worth the living."

If, throughout the land, we were frankly to say: "We have been unintelligent and inefficient; we have been wasteful of time and resources. Let's buck up now and see how we can do things differently," it might have a powerful effect upon the morale of our people. For basically the vast majority of us are in love with the free processes of democracy. Freedom is in the blood of us. But also most of us are fairly astute. If democratic freedom continues to land us in intolerable economic, political, and social confusion—and if we are told that patriotism requires that we shut our eyes to this fact—we are practical-minded enough to say, "Let's have less freedom and more successful action."

## II

There is a second weakness in our defense. Americans have lived through an age of industrial and financial expansion. So powerful have the industrial and financial enterprisers been that they have practically taken us over. In a thousand ways they have come to own America. In a thousand ways they dominate the lives of Americans. Increasingly we have resented this. We have put up with it because of the incidental benefits that have accrued to us. But deeply we have resented the transformation of our democracy into a near-plutocracy. We have watched the long process of the money-corruption of our legislatures and courts of law. We have seen cities bought and sold. We have seen the honest processes of democracy flouted and set at naught. And, worst of all, we have seen our people, time and again, fooled into supporting with their lives financial interests when they thought they were supporting democratic freedom.

These interests are not inactive today. We are suspicious of them. And yet we do not quite know how to get on the track of them. We are desperately afraid that once more a war will be started ostensibly for the defense of democracy, but actually for defense of the moneybags.

This is what divides the minds of our people. Were it a clean-cut issue of defending the freedom of man against the barbaric destruction of that freedom, we should all, at once, spring to arms. But we are not so sure but that when the call to arms comes it will be only to perpetuate an outworn system of special privilege that continues to defeat the democracy we care about. We have been fooled in so many economic and political shell games that we prefer to watch a while longer to see whether this is not another.

An obligation for the defense of America rests squarely upon the shoulders of our privileged classes. They have to make it clear to us—clear beyond the shadow of a doubt—that they care more about the freedom of all of us than about their own profits. It was the privileged classes that sold out France. They preferred to lose France rather than to lose some of their money and power. They were more afraid of the social reforms of Premier Blum than they were of the despotic barbarities of Hitler.

Our privileged classes in America have to make a clear confession of their intentions. Only yesterday one of our top industrialists spoke to his fellow industrialists and financiers. What he said should send shivers down the spine of every American who is enlisting for this new fight for freedom. Be it remembered that he was talking to his fellow industrialists and financiers, and not to the American people. What he is reported to have told them is that wages must not be permitted to go up as fast as the cost of living, and that overtime must no longer be paid for at an extra rate! An old order speaking to an old order. But more than this, a dominant industrialist prepared—in the same old way—to take advantage of the patriotic preoccupations of his countrymen to strike one further blow at the laboring man!

Perhaps it is too much to ask that Bourbons cease to be Bourbons. Privilege breeds arrogance and insensitivity. It breeds the passion for more privilege. But if America is to be defended by a unified people, it must not be betrayed by an arrogant and insensitive few.

Another member of the privileged classes is reported to have said recently that the time is now ripe for the "better people" to hold their own against "the masses." This was not democracy speaking. This is what has kept democracy from being fulfilled. And this is what, if we are not alert, will sell us out to our enemies.

We know that there are many liberals among the financially privileged—men and women who feel that the time has come for a different and more generous ordering of life and who would gladly give up a major portion of their own possessions if they knew how to do this in ways that would further the common good. The tragedy is that these men and women are so largely inarticulate. They do not make proclamations. They go modestly on their way doing good where they see the chance to do it. They do not organize to set before the public their conception of what our American Tomorrow is to be. Unfortunately, then, they are too often labeled by the same labels that fit their less generous fellows-in-privilege. It might be an excellent and triumphant thing for all of us if these honest stewards of property were to speak up for themselves, declare their intentions, let us know where they stand, so that we could all feel them as a part of the fellowship that is looking ahead.

## III

There is another weakness in our defenses. Hitler is moving over into America. The meanest of all his views is taking root among us. It is a shameful thing to contemplate. But the vicious anti-Semitism whereby he roused the furies in his own people is making its way into America. The "nice people" are beginning subtly to indicate their distaste of Jews. We remember a number of years ago the reports of Henry Ford's attempted crusade against the Jewish people. It would seem, from various sources, that he and his men have not ceased to carry on that crusade. By subtle insinuation and by support of anti-Semitic leaders, he and his chief representatives are said to be carrying on an effort to stir up race hatred. It is ironic to find Mr. Ford supporting the Reverend Mr. Buchman's Oxford Movement for Moral Rearmament. "Moral Rearmament," he is quoted as saying in a pamphlet issued by the Movement, "gives me hope for the future of our country and the world." And he goes on to say, "There is enough good will in the people to overcome all war, all class dissension, all economic stagnation, when that good will shall be hitched to the affairs of men and nations." Excellent words, but how do they comport with an apparent effort to stir up hatred against the Jewish people? Good will in a democracy means good will toward all, or it means ill will toward some. When ill will toward some becomes the established policy of a people, then farewell democracy.

There is a devastating power in Hitler's technique of repeated assertion. He tells the world—and keeps telling the world over and over—that the Jews have been the cause of all our troubles. People who are ignorant of social cause and effect keep hearing this; and eventually they begin to believe it. This is what may be happening in our country. We do not find that people who are intelligent about social cause and effect, people who have dug deep into the reasons for our troubles, take the short and easy and stupid way of anti-Semitism. They know how preposterous the assertion is that the Jews have caused everything that is reprehensible. They know the assertion to be a red herring drawn across the path of the real causes of our difficulties. But ignorant people—and, sad to say, it is not only the poor who are ignorant; many of our wealthiest people are densely ignorant of history and culture—are taken in by this vicious falsifying of facts.

Hitler's technique of endless repetition is having its effect in America. In a Southern city a large evangelistic tent had this banner over the entrance: "The Jews Killed Our Christ. Why Should We Not Kill the Jews?" This is one way in which anti-Semitism rears its head among the poorer classes; but here is another story. The program chairman of a woman's club recently went to a lecture bureau to secure a speaker on contemporary events. She was given the name of a distinguished historian, who is also a Jew. The woman looked shocked. "Oh, no," she exclaimed. "I couldn't go back to my club and tell them I had engaged a Jew." A small straw, but it shows the way the wind may be blowing.

What is happening in America? Are we becoming convinced that, even in this most unmerciful and libelous aspect of his efficiency, Hitler is right? Are we prepared to surrender the generosity of a Lincoln to the mean littleness of this hate-spitting Austrian tyrant?

Here is a weakness in our defenses. How are we going, with all the strength of our passion, to oppose a man whose views we covertly approve? All too late, we learned that within the European democracies were hosts of Quislings who sincerely admired the Hitler philosophy. Are we breeding Quislings in our own midst?

One line of our defense must be a strong assertion on the part of every one of us that anti-Semitism is utterly and irrevocably anti-American.

We need that assertion to be made as profoundly as we need a salute to the flag. The Quislings are always able to salute. Doubtless, too, they will be able to say in public that they love the Jews. Nevertheless, a widespread reassertion on the part of all of us that democracy can have no commerce with racial hatred, that anti-Semitism is anti-Americanism, might help to stiffen our resolution and cause these disbelievers in the democratic ideal to watch their step.

These are some of the weak places in our defense: the absence of a profound and searching self-criticism of our American way of doing things; the absence among our privileged classes of a frank expression of willingness to risk even their profits for the defense of freedom; the growing presence in our midst of the ugly racial intolerances that have made the Hitler philosophy the most detestable in all history. As we confront a difficult future we shall have to come fully and honestly to terms with ourselves along all these lines. We shall have to be a stronger people than we are today, a people more united in common understanding and confidence in one another, if we are to save what we care about.

★ *4* ★

# THE POWER OF TRUTH

## I

HOWEVER many mistakes our civilization may have made, it has held to one strong belief—that truth is the way of man's salvation. Our civilization has not always known the truth; knowing the truth, it has not always followed it. But deeper than all other convictions has been this one, that the way of life, if it is to lead to happiness, must be the way of truth. "Ye shall know the truth, and the truth shall set you free." This has been in the blood of us. It has been the cornerstone of every school, every college, every university. It has been the foundation of the sciences, of medicine, and of every technological art. To base our life on falsehood, we have believed, is to hasten our life toward self-destruction.

We stand aghast, then, at a concerted effort to make the disinterested search for truth a mortal offense. Nothing that has happened in the totalitarian countries has shown more deeply the viciousness of their ideology than the attempt to fabricate truth for the sake of party success. Germans are always thorough. In this case they have been the most thorough of all. They have ruled out the long researches of scientists and fabricated a race view of their own. They have fabricated their own history, retelling the story of Christianity to suit Nazi aims, retelling the story of the German past to make it fit the aims of a Nazi present. They have turned schools into the agencies of party propaganda and universities into research laboratories for the distortion of facts to support Nazi theses. Professors in Germany are not servants of the truth. They are servants of the Nazi state. They do not think; they follow command. It is significant that at one of the great universities—hitherto proud of its devotion to accurate scholarship—the statue of Minerva, Goddess of Wisdom, was taken down from over the portal and the symbol of Nazism put in its place. Mathematics must be Nazi mathematics; biology, Nazi biology; anthropology, Nazi anthropology.

The whole thing would be ludicrous were it not an actual fact. Here is a land whose rulers have said: "Ye shall know lies, and lies shall set you free."

We Americans need to think hard about this. There is something beguiling about Hitler's statement that Europe is to be remade, and that an old order of economics and politics is to be transformed into a new and better order. We all want Europe remade. Most of us—the alert-minded among us—want the old order of economics and politics transformed into a new and better one. But with Hitler's words go his deeds. In order to remake Europe, he kills the truth. In order to transform an old order into a new, he sets falsehood on high.

This cannot be the American way. We began our career as a people by saying: "We hold these truths to be self-evident." We honestly believed they were truths. We have never yet discovered that Thomas Jefferson was a Minister of Propaganda hired to galvanize Colonials by lies into support of the Revolutionary cause. He believed the words he wrote were truths. We believed they were truths. And because we so believed, we were strong to defend them.

In a number of ways we have built our national life on the honest search for truth. One of our first significant enterprises was to establish a public-school system. It was never permitted to be the instrument of a party, nor of the state. The American public-school system has been free not only in the sense that it has been open to everyone, but in the sense that it has been politically uncommanded. It has not taught American mathematics, nor Republican-party mathematics, nor Democratic-party mathematics, but mathematics. So with biology, anthropology, and the rest.

This had been our pride. Our schools have indeed fallen down in many ways; they have not been free from the pressure of the political and economic mores; but they have never quite fallen to the low estate of being instruments for the propaganda of a party. Poor as they may have been, they have, in their intent, been in the service of truth.

Let Nazism sweep this country, and we must close these schools. We must close our colleges and universities. We must turn out honesty and turn in dishonesty. Our teachers must follow command. They must goosestep their minds to falsehoods fabricated by their party superiors.

Another of our American enterprises was to establish a free press. It was not easy sledding; and even today our press is not wholly free. But there is still in us the vigorous will to make it free. For we know that a kept press means a kept people; and we Americans long ago decided that we were going to be a free people.

In totalitarian countries journalism is a tragedy. Reporters see what they are told to see, report what they are told to report. The public does not get news; it gets views. It gets the fabrications that a determined set of men thinks necessary in order to arouse passions and stiffen courage for the support of their ends. The press is a tool for enslavement, not for liberation.

A new order of life does, indeed, need to be created. Our shackled civilization needs to be set free. But organized falsehood—persistent and all-embracing—can never set it free. The spirit that is democracy calls for a different way.

## II

What is to be our defense against this lifting of the lie into a place of power? The answer should be clear. The only lasting and powerful defense against falsehood is truth. We Americans have to cultivate a new seriousness about truth.

While we have never had a national policy of deliberate falsification—although secret diplomacy came perilously near to that—we have not been slow to employ all kinds of special lies in all kinds of special areas. For a long time advertising was an area of expected lying. It is not so now—or at least almost not so. Truthtelling has proved itself to be more successful. But business practices, on the whole, are not yet free from the use of deception. Short-weighting the customer is not unknown among us; passing him an inferior article as if it were a superior; labeling a product in such a way as to make him think he is getting what he is not getting (buy a package marked "cinnamon," and you will find in *very* small letters that it is not cinnamon at all but a cheap substitute—so named, however, that you do not know it is a cheap substitute); selling a customer a woolen suit that is mostly shoddy; financing his car under a contract that binds him to obligations he knows nothing about and would not undertake if he knew; building him a house that skimps on specifications—such instances can be repeated indefinitely. Thousands of small lies in business practices have become so much the expected thing that a man would be a naïve innocent who did not watch out for them. But not only are these deceptions expected; they are even condoned. "Everybody's doing it." "That's what business has to be." "You've got to expect it." We are easygoing about it; but psychologically we have built ourselves into a people who do not trust one another, into a people constantly on guard lest they be "gypped." Business practices are better today than they used to be; but they will have to be much better if the American people are to have confidence in one another as individuals whose "word is their bond."

Again the law is notoriously an area where the layman, particularly the layman of small means, expects to be cheated somewhere along the line. Lawyers have woven words into such intricacies of bewildering and ambiguous patterns that it is no trouble at all for them to make the false appear to be the true. Lawyers even joke about their own untrustworthiness. A well-known lawyer is reported recently to have said (speaking to his colleagues): "If the evidence is against you, appeal to the law; if the law is against you, appeal to the evidence; if both are against you, stand up and yell like hell!" And we remember the cynical remark: "Law begins in ideals and ends in deals." The law has its large share of responsibility for the lack of confidence that Americans have in one another—lack of confidence in the honest intentions of our corporations; lack of confidence in the vaunted principle of "equality before the law." Law has to clean its house of lies and paid liars before there can be full confidence in the legal processes on the part of the American people.

Politics is still a royal field for lying. To be sure, much of the lying—at election times particularly—is obvious and a joke. But much of it reaches deep into the foundations of our lives, unsettling those foundations. The oh-so-virtuous public mask of the city mayor or the state senator or the governor, and behind it the brain busy with rackets and rake-offs—this is commonplace in America. It does not make good recalling. It should make us uneasy in these days of national crisis. We are to defend America? With all these rats in public office?

Even education—hard as we have tried to keep it honest—comes in for its share of dishonesty. In recent years, eminent historians have tried to wean us away from the fairy-tale accounts of American history. They have tried to tell us the actual facts about our past. Has this honesty been well received? All over the country vigorous, even violent, opposition has developed. "These men are dirtying our American past!" "They are libeling our forefathers!" One woman in an Eastern city is reported to have shrilled: "They want our children to read unbiased history. How can we give our children unbiased facts if we want them to keep their ideals?" The whole thing would be funny did it not point to a deep lack of confidence in truth. American history, it seems, needs to be "dressed up." It needs to be told in such fashion as to "encourage patriotism." Honest, realistic truth is not good enough for that! We have to give our children—and ourselves—romantic fictions. One is tempted to ask, with the poet Robinson,[1]

> What has truth done to us
> That we must always be afraid of it . . . ?

[1] E. A. Robinson, "Nicodemus," *Collected Poems* (New York: Macmillan & Co.), p. 1166.

We are seeing today what Hitler's lies can do to a people and what they threaten to do to our world. There is no alternative for us: we Americans will have to get a new grip on truth—truth in business, truth in law, truth in politics, truth in education. In a multitude of unnoticed ways we have woven a social fabric with threads of lies running through it. They are not pretty to look at. They do not strengthen the fabric.

Our next job as a people will have to be to learn a new respect for truth, for only the truth-attitudes of a truth-caring people can make us strong.

# 5

# THE THING WE CALL EFFICIENCY

## I

THE "historical spirit," the Nazis assert, indicates "with apodictic certainty" that the future is not with democracy. Democracy, they tell us, is too soft, too fumbling, too inefficient, to survive. The future is with the disciplined peoples, the peoples that are willing to forego their rights of endless palaver and follow command; that prefer the power which comes from collective obedience to the powerlessness that stems from mass liberty.

There is just enough truth in what these menacing newcomers say about the weakness of democracy to make us take a searching look at ourselves. Perhaps this thing we have called democracy is not nearly so perfect as we have thought. Perhaps we have liked it chiefly because it caters to our conceit (it tells even the stupidest that he is "equal" to the others); or because it lets us be lazily irresponsible (it tells us we are "free"). It demands nothing of us except an occasional visit to the polls. If it taxes us too unpleasantly, we exercise our democratic right to shout to the high heavens—and there is pleasure in that. If it asks us, the strong ones, not to exploit our weaker fellows, we tell it to "keep hands off," that we are the people as much as anyone else, and that we have, and intend to keep, all the rights and privileges that go with free enterprise in a democracy.

It may be that we like democracy chiefly because it does not interfere with us. We like it as children like indulgent grandparents, who let them run wild, eat what they please, stay up way beyond bedtime.

Government has always been a pretty distasteful thing to most of us. It is the agency which commands and forbids. We experience government first in the form of parents—in the morning when we want to sleep, in the daytime when we want to play, at night when we want to stay up. Then we experience it in the form of teachers; then in the form of policemen and tax collectors, lawmakers and judges. Government, whether in the family, the school, or the state, goes counter to our natural inclinations. Some of us dislike its restrictions so heartily that we spend prodigious energy devising means to escape them. All of us, when we consult our natural inclinations, feel that "the less government the better." So democracy, where there is least government of all, becomes for us a kind of social paradise.

The child in us, however, has to grow up: our natural inclinations have to be disciplined into social will and ordered living. Perhaps democracy has been an illusion of freedom. Perhaps we of the democracies need to grow up to a sturdier and harder, more disciplined and obedient, less free, but in the end more characterful, way of life.

Where does the truth lie? Which way of life will be strongest to survive?

## II

Whatever the answer may be, we of the democracies will have to begin by making a frank confession of our sins. It will do us no good to shout back at the Nazis, in Sandburg's ironic words, that "we are the greatest people . . . nothing like us ever was." This would be adolescent. We shall exhibit our maturity best by frankly admitting that democracy has suffered from profound weaknesses. It has, without question, been altogether too much government—and misgovernment—by palaver; it has been government that has all too frequently given liberty the right to be license; it has been a way of life that has made it easy for the strong to plunder the weak; it has been far too generally freedom without responsibility. These weaknesses, and a great many others, we shall have frankly to admit. The admission will enable us to start from scratch. But it will also assure us that while democratic freedom has tempted us into many failures, it has not taken from us this one essential of sound life: the power to survey ourselves with critical honesty.

Basically, the issue is not between democracy *as it is* (with its many failures) and Nazism *as it expects to become* (when it has fulfilled its promises). The issue, more deeply, is between what democracy can become and what Nazism can become. Which of these, in all its potentials, is the stronger to survive?

We have to go deep into human nature to answer this question. We need to understand what develops people most fully, what releases their energies, tightens their wills, gives zest and resistlessness to their purposes. Most important of all, we need to know how much margin for error is essential, if the human spirit is to be given its fullest chance.

Let us consider the second point first, for it is probably the most fundamental. . . . Appearances sometimes deceive us. When the first awkward contraptions called horseless carriages were staggering and rattling their way over rough country roads, it looked for all the world as if they were the most inefficient mechanisms ever devised by men. Compared with the shining efficiency of a four-horse coach, they were ludicrous. It was no wonder that as these stuttering, disjointed contraptions stalled on the roads, farmers, sweeping by in their buggies, shouted derisively, "Get a horse!" But the clumsy contraptions embodied a way of life—one that was to win out in the end. That way of life was the way of fumbling trial and error. If in the first years of automobile research someone had suggested that it would be far more efficient to appoint an automobile dictator, who would give the authoritative word as to how automobiles were to be built, the powerful machine of today would never have materialized. At that time there was no single man, nor group of men, who "with apodictic certainty" could have said how a gas-propelled machine should be built. Many minds had to fumble, to try and fail, to look utterly ludicrous in their failures, before the secret could be discovered. It was needful, in short, that there should be a large margin for error.

This is the deepest essential of effective, progressive human life—the right to make mistakes, and the right progressively and peacefully to correct mistakes. Animals possess this only in slight degree. They, in their narrow ways, are utterly efficient. Almost from birth, they are all there, streamlined for action. But because they are all there, they never get anywhere else. Having no margin for fumbling, for trying out new ways, they remain set in their ancestral pattern. They are utterly efficient and utterly fixed.

The Nazis recognize this in the area of mechanical inventions, just as we do. But they repudiate it in the far more difficult, because subtler and more complicated, areas of social invention. They take it for granted that in these areas there need be no fumbling, no trying of this and then that. They shout derisively at the stuttering, staggering, stalling democracies, "Get a Leader!" They assume that a Leader can be found who can show us how to take the infinitely delicate, maddeningly stubborn, bewilderingly unpredictable elements of a human society and so assemble them as to make a perfect social machine.

They presume to take from us, as *social* beings, the one power that is both our weakness and our strength. They permit mechanical trial and error, but insist upon social certainty.

All good thinking is long-range thinking. The Nazis think at short range. For the time being, they can whip a society into a semblance of unity; they can make individuals in that society go delirious with the will to obey; they can build a consolidated strength, and hurl that strength at other peoples. But they do their short-range thinking at the terrible cost of surrendering the one power that at all times and in all places has made man the forward-going animal.

## III

Our second point has to do with what "starts the wheels going" in us, and keeps them going. Two psychological principles are at war in the world today: that of order and that of initiative. The Nazis have chosen order as of primary worth; the democracies, initiative.

Order, in the human world, connotes obedience. It connotes the willingness to be a part of a whole and to play the part assigned.

Sparta was built on the principle of order. As a state, it was a vast military formation, with hierarchy of ranks, sharply defined duties for each rank, with command and obedience as the animating spirit. Sparta was a strong state, but it produced nothing but military strength—and that only for a brief period. Through later history we remember it only as walls of soldiers. Nothing else remains of it. The Spartan state condemned itself to the mortal weakness of being so powerfully organized that it could do only the one thing it set out to do. That one thing—being strong—was so small a part of what man has it in him to be that the Spartan contribution to our human adventure is now merely an ugly memory.

Order is good; but order, it would seem, is never enough. Even the ordered rendition of an orchestra has back of it the creative efforts of the composer. To make order vital and progressive, something deeper and more powerful than order is required. The democracies seem to have got hold of this deeper requirement. They recognize that man cannot live by command alone. For them, it still remains true that the spirit bloweth where it listeth. Where the spirit of man is taken sternly and efficiently in hand, and bidden to blow through prearranged wind tunnels, its errant genius dies. Man is a creature born to be free in his imaginings and contrivings, and any order of life which, by a total plan, admonishes him how his imaginings and contrivances are to go, would seem to condemn itself to sterility.

Nazism, in short, is a peculiarly perverted, short-range view of human nature. It is as perverted and short-ranged as the view of ancient pedagogues who, for their own convenience, instilled knowledge with a rod. In the presence of those ancient functionaries, no child disobeyed; but also no child had a chance to grow into the generous fullness of his powers. The democracies have a better view of human nature, albeit they fail deplorably at times to live up to it. Their view assumes in all individuals hidden powers that should be released. They are not presumptuous enough to believe that any one person knows beforehand what powers are there and what should be released. Because they know they do not know, they refuse to lay the rough hand of the State upon the souls of its people.

Nazism is fatally presumptuous because it assumes a knowledge of human impulses and aspirations no mortal can have, and a control no mortal should possess. And so, in the long run, it would seem, Nazism must go the way of death, since it denies in man that which is the way of life. Democracy may be foolish and fumbling. At times it may be maddeningly inefficient; but it still seems true that its way is the way of life.

But while democracy may be strong in principle, in practice, as we have said, it may be profoundly weak. For democracy is not something that runs itself. It has to be run by people—not by a few of them, but, strange as this may seem, by all. Democracy is what its people are; and people are the way they think and feel and act. It will not do for the educated people in a democracy to shrug their shoulders at the "ignorance of the masses." If the masses are ignorant, wisdom in high places will have hard sledding. Nor will it do for them to pass over lightly the fact that the "classes" think mainly of their own interests. If the "classes" continue to think mainly of their own interests, they will be ill prepared to defend government of and by and for the people.

Democracy's line of defense is within the minds and spirits of all its people. Either these minds and spirits must be alive with purposes that are genuinely good for all and firm with courage to carry out these purposes, or democracy will go down before forces alert to what they want and powerfully equipped—for the present, at least—to get what they want.

# 6

# HOW DEMOCRACY MUST PROVE ITS CASE

## I

WHEN, in their state of original nature, men are free to do as they please, what they please to do is to fight one another. This was what the philosopher Hobbes believed. So he reached his political conclusion: men have to surrender their liberties to the coercive power of government in order to protect themselves against themselves.

It was a curious theory; but, interpreted in a certain way, it had in it an element of truth. If by the "original nature of men" we mean their unadorned and unmitigated selfishness, Hobbes was right. Sheer selfishness cannot be permitted to possess sheer freedom. The strong arm of authority must have power to curb freedom when freedom has no impulse except to serve itself. What is questionable about Hobbes's view is its assumption that men in their original nature are unmitigatedly selfish.

American democracy was founded on a more generous conception of human nature. It was based on a belief, not in the original selfishness of men, but in their original decency. Those who drew up the plans for our democracy were more inclined to believe that men were made evil by government than that government was needed to protect men against the evil in themselves. These founders of our democracy had seen too much of the mischief wrought by kings and oligarchies to be enamored of the view that strong, coercive government is the way of man's salvation.

Knowing well what governments had done to people, they were rather convinced that if people could only be allowed to go their free ways, attending to their own affairs, given the opportunity to bring those affairs to fruition, the inherent decency in them would assert itself. They would, by common consent, institute such government among themselves as was needed to carry on their common concerns. Such government, however, would not be a coercive limitation of their liberty but rather a carrying out of their joint will to do the things they freely willed to do.

Our democracy was rooted in this more generous view of human nature. It regarded man as basically not a creature of evil intent, but of good intent. Give him scope, give him freedom to be what he inherently desires to be, cease thwarting him, angering him, torturing him, and he will freely build a society in which free men can live in the peace of mutual helpfulness and respect.

When this theory was promulgated to the world, it was regarded as sheerest folly. It went counter to all the traditions. Christian religion had taken it for granted that men were born in sin and needed to be watched by a jealous God. The social and political philosophies of Europe had assumed as a matter of course that the masses of people were stupid and selfish, and for their own good needed to be ruled by a divinely selected few. All the traditions were against this upstart view that men are basically decent, and, if given freedom to work out their destinies, will work them out in ways that are good for all. The sophisticates of the world laughed our naïve psychological generosity to scorn.

Times have changed, however, and true sophistication seems to be on the side of this bold belief of ours. A more informed psychology than was possible in those days has taught us that most of the evils from which men suffer are the evils, not of freedom, but of compulsion. Psychological wisdom today consists in showing how to release into freedom the inherent urgencies of man. This does not mean that discipline and restraint are of no importance. It means, however, that the wisest discipline and the wisest restraint are achieved not when they are coerced, but when they are self-enacted. "Free men set themselves free." [1] The discipline of free men is self-discipline; their restraint is self-restraint.

Today another social and political philosophy arises to dispute the claims of this view of human nature which sees in self-disciplined freedom the best way of life. Hobbes, viewing man in his original selfishness, as nasty, brutish, and forever at war with his fellow men, wished, through government, to coerce him into peace. This new philosophy that begins to bestride the world, wishes, through government, to coerce him into the spirit and activity of war. For war, this view declares, is the true ennobler of man. It ennobles because it requires the surrender of the individual will to the total will. War is the most effective way in which man is helped out of his persistent selfishness and made into a creature of wider loyalty. The object of government, so this new view holds, should be to regiment men into the spirit and service of war.

It is a curious view; it, too, regarded from a certain angle, has its element of truth. If, by the human being, one means the human being in his usual condition of

[1] James Oppenheim, "The Slave," *Collected Poems* (New York: Alfred A. Knopf).

present-day life—harassed by petty concerns for a livelihood, insecure, anxious, competing with his fellows—one is not describing a greatly noble creature. Let there now be a call to arms, and this far from noble creature is suddenly transformed. He sinks his petty will in the will of the total group. He loses himself—and finds himself.

This new view, therefore, which seeks to coerce men into the heroic warlike way of life, has its partial justification. The average circumstances of life today do not release the inherent nobility of men. They hold men, rather, to levels of self-interest and self-concern. To this extent, then, the new philosophy is correct. We need to find ways of releasing the more-than-self-centered in men. We need to discover how to change the petty, anxious, self-interested individual of today into one who can devote himself willingly and bravely to something greater than himself.

Hobbes thought that men needed to be coerced into peace. Totalitarianism thinks that men need to be coerced into war. Both lacked confidence in man's power to ennoble his life through freedom. Only democracy clings to the belief that, given freedom enough, man will achieve the greatness he has it in him to achieve.

This democratic philosophy, however, of fulfillment through freedom, has to do more than announce itself as true. In the skeptical world of today, it has to prove its truth by the test of its people's behavior. It may quite properly be urged against democracy that freedom has not worked out as beautifully as was first expected. "Liberty for all" has allowed strong individuals to oppose the weak. It has opened the doors to all manner of clever dishonesty, in private and public life.

Viewing the many failures of democracy, we are compelled to ask ourselves whether we have not gone too far in permitting men to be free. Perhaps they are not yet ready for the freedom which democracy grants them. Perhaps they need to be restrained for their own good as well as for the good of others. Freedom, in short, may be too dangerous a privilege to grant to such imperfect beings as we still are.

These doubts may not be brushed aside. They have to be resolved. For the facts are not yet all in. Democracy, in America as elsewhere, is still in the making. It has not yet proved its case. Hence its role in the world today is not to declare itself, dogmatically, to be the true way of life. Its role is, rather, humbly and searchingly to prove that it can become the true way of life.

This places upon the free people of a democracy a profound obligation. They have to use their freedom in ways which prove that freedom works. If, given wide liberties, they use them ungenerously to the injury of their fellow men, they help to prove the case against democracy. But if, given wide liberties, they use these with increasing generosity, they, to that extent, help to prove the case for democracy.

## II

There are at least four kinds of generosity required of free people if freedom is to prove its case.

The first is generosity about ideas. The essence of democracy is the belief that ideas have no privileged origin. They do not need to come from king or class. They are as likely as not to come from the humblest individual in the land. Ideas are born out of the freedom of man's spirit. This is why a free people cannot abide the thought that one man or group of men should be accorded the exclusive right to the ideas that should govern. This, too, is why a free people believe in the right of everyone to express his ideas.

But it takes self-discipline to practice this. Sometimes our own ideas seem to be the very voice of truth itself, while dissenting ideas seem the very antithesis of everything decent people care about. Shall we permit these evil ideas to be spread among us, perverting the minds of our people? There come times when it seems a wholly righteous thing to tear this man from the platform, to break up his meeting, to run him out of our presence. What he says is dangerous, is it not? Shall we suffer our people to be misled? If he is a teacher, teaching views that we hold to be anathema, have we not the right to bid him cease, to demand that he resign his position? Who is he to set himself up against the opinions of honest Americans?

The story of the suppression of free speech in America is an ominous one. It is the story of American democracy not yet come of age, the story of democracy time after time stupidly defeating itself. I have a letter which has just come to hand from a schoolteacher in a Western city. It might have come from almost any city in America, and might have been written at almost any time in recent years: "The Forums have moved along with vigor so far—audiences and speakers good and not so good. There has been much commotion, however, in the 'Readers' Viewpoint' column about the lecture schedule for Professor —. The district attorney wrote that Professor — had Communistic tendencies, and that he should not be allowed, and that no one from his office should go to the lecture. A Mr. —, who has a personal grudge against the chairman because the chairman will not permit him to surround his questions from the floor with a lecture, took up the district attorney's objection and wrote that public funds should not be used to bring in a Red speaker."

I happen to know the man to whom they are objecting. He is an honest, militant opponent of economic privilege and a courageous defender of liberal labor policies. And he happens not to be a Communist. He has every right to believe as he does—and is probably right in most of his beliefs. Yet in that Western city an official of our democracy and a disgruntled citizen head a movement to close his mouth.

On the very same morning on which this letter arrived, the foreign news section of the newspaper carried the account of a proposed agreement between the Vichy government and the Axis powers for a common effort toward the reorganization of Europe. In the account was the warning that *no newspaper in France was to criticize this proposed agreement.*

In France they now close the mouths of their people. In this Western city American citizens would close the mouth of a fellow American.

Let this become more than an isolated incident, let it become the habit of Americans to deny freedom of speech to those whose views they dislike, and American democracy will cease to survive. The most dangerous thing that is happening among us today is the liberty taken by irresponsible Americans—individually and in groups—to deny liberty to people whom they detest. It now takes the patriotic form of ferreting out Fifth Columnists. But not everyone who shouts "Fifth Columnist" will have found one. As likely as not he will be venting his spite against someone who has stood in his way. It has been suggested that we need to add another Column to the enemies of democracy —the Sixth Column—composed of those who, in the name of patriotism, sound the alarm against everything that is socially, politically, or economically liberal.

Democracies, we have learned of late, may not have to be defeated from without; they can disintegrate from within. Our own democracy begins to disintegrate the moment we cease to be generous to the free expression of ideas. Even if ideas are dangerous, the expression of them must be permitted, for the suppression of them is infinitely more dangerous than the ideas themselves. Their suppression marks the surrender of democracy. Their expression merely requires that we be vigilant enough to detect their falsity. As a recent writer has said: "We have to fight for democracy with democracy." We cannot fight for the right to be a society of free minds by first denying the right of free minds to be free. Democracy requires of us the difficult self-discipline of giving to everyone the right to say his say. But it requires also the equally difficult self-discipline of becoming intelligent enough to distinguish truth from falsity.

## III

The second generosity required in a democracy is generosity about backgrounds. The proudest boast of our country is that it has been formed out of the peoples of the world, out of rich and poor, out of the high in station and the low, out of people of all creeds and races. American freedom has never presupposed a family tree, a butler in the hall, or a card of racial purity. America has believed that all individuals, as individuals, have the right to participate in the processes and rewards of democratic life.

The dictators regard this view with scorn. They have arrogantly set up a master-slave society where correct racial origin is prerequisite to entrance into rulership and rewards. In so doing, they have set up the very antithesis of a society of free minds. In a society of free minds, racial discrimination can have no place.

Here, again, there is required of us a difficult self-discipline. It is easy to feel that *our* race, *our* sect, is the best. This is the persistent ethnocentrism in us. It is hard to believe that men and women of different race and background should have the same basic value and rights as we. Note how hard it is for us to be generous to Negroes. Even in a society dedicated to the freedom of all, we still keep colored people socially, economically, and often politically unfree. Only the finer minds among us have as yet achieved the self-discipline that makes race no ban to full respect and full opportunity.

The discipline which a free society requires is the discipline of our racial snobbishnesses. We must not blow hot and cold in this matter. Either we support a generous view of human nature, or subtly we prepare the way for the ruthlessness of racial hoodlumism.

## IV

The third generosity required of us is generosity about life-opportunity. In a democracy we have to *want* life-opportunity for everyone. This, however, is easier said than done. It takes a high order of mind to care deeply about whether other people have the chances they should have. Chiefly, it takes imagination; and imagination is rare. Imagination, in the case of people, is the power to get the "image" of them that they have of themselves. It is the power to penetrate beneath their skins and think and feel as they do.

This imaginative power is required in the people of

a democracy because if it is lacking they are easily insensitive to the needs of other people, even ruthless about these needs. One's interest in one's own affairs is always enough to keep one fully occupied. If one lacks imagination about other people, one sees them as little more than perambulating bundles of skin and bone; and about such perambulating bundles it is difficult to become greatly concerned. To use Nietzsche's phrase, there are "much too many" of them. While, in words, one grants that there should be, among all people, equal opportunity for life, liberty, and the pursuit of happiness, in actual practice each one attends to the opportunities he himself can capture.

This, however, is not enough. Democracy is distinguished from all other forms of life by its belief in the equal rights of all to opportunity. This equality of rights, however, does not become automatically established. The people of a democracy have to establish it. This requires of a democratic people imagination about their fellows and a will to create opportunities that answer to their needs.

Difficult and rare as this imaginative power is, it can be said, I think, to be growing among us. We are a people increasingly aware of the rest of the people around us. In recent decades we have been seeing more and more what people need if their lives are to become fulfilled. They need air and sunshine. Parks and playgrounds are signs of our aroused imagination. They need food and shelter. Public health education, pure food laws, public housing projects are signs of an awakened imagination. They need security and self-respect in the making of a livelihood. Here, too, our imagination is alive. We support movements for the raising of wage levels, for shorter hours, for the bettering of work conditions, for collective bargaining, for unemployment insurance, for the support of old age.

This awakening of the imagination of our people is all part of the maturing process through which our democracy is passing. On the other hand, to the extent that individuals among us are still insensitive to the needs of their fellows and through that insensitivity diminish their life-opportunities, they constitute a hindrance to the development of a free society and are a weakness in its defense.

## V

The fourth generosity required of us is generosity about other peoples of the world. Racial snobbishness is bad; national snobbishness is equally so. A free people must want all other peoples to be free. I have heard Americans say of the European nations: "Let them stew in their own juice." An excuse might be made for momentary exasperation on our part. There is little in recent European behavior to give us confidence. And yet we as a free people have to remember that Europe is more than governments. It is people—honest, friendly, hard-working people. Of recent years, the furious fanaticism of power-seeking leaders has turned many of these honest, friendly, hard-working people into furious fanatics. But it has left others of them saddened and bewildered. Europe is neither wholly good nor wholly bad. If we let Europe stew in its own juice, if we stand aside and thank God that we are not as Europeans are, we give up the grandest part of our American dream, which is to help make the world a decent place for people to live in.

We still have a job that goes beyond the borders of our own land. Once we invited the oppressed of the world to come to us. We still invite a few of them; but we cannot invite many. Now our greater job is to go out to the oppressed of the world.

To many, this sounds fantastic. Our American job, they tell us, is to stay at home and mind our own affairs. If this means that we should not join in the mad military furies of the Europeans, it is true. But there are other ways of going abroad than sending expeditionary forces.

Somehow and somewhen a sane unity of the world

will have to be created. Competitive nationalism of the nineteenth-century sort is in its death throes. The new world that is coming into being will require something far better than the traditional aggressivenesses of sovereign nations.

The American who cares about freedom will have to discipline his mind to a new way of thinking. He will have to pass beyond his easy, confident localism and learn to think in world terms. This will be a much harder way for him to think, for the world patterns are still unformed. But if he cares about making freedom grow in strength and grandeur, he will have to accustom himself to think in this broader way. The day for provincial Americanism is past. To save the freedom of America, we shall have somehow to help achieve the freedom of the peoples of the world.

These are four ways of generosity that are prerequisite to the continuance and the strong defense of a society of free people–generosity about ideas, about the backgrounds of people, about life-opportunity, and about other peoples of the world. They all root in a fundamental respect for human beings, in the conviction that all human beings should have full access to the resources of life. This is democracy's way. We defend democracy best as we discipline ourselves for the achievement of this way of life.

Part Two

# OLD HABITS TO REJECT

## ★ 7 ★

# STRAIGHTENING OUT OUR LOGIC

## I

WHEN an old order changes, we have to change with it, or the logic of our life is broken. To hold to old ways when new ways demand us is to live a contradiction. We of the present generation have to prepare ourselves for the shaping of a new America as part of a new civilization. Only minds completely stultified, by habit or by an absorbed self-interest, can any longer believe that we shall some day—at home and abroad—return to "normalcy." New conditions have come which require new arrangements; these new arrangements require new outlooks on our part, new loyalties, and new efforts.

We shall be ill prepared to defend ourselves if we are prepared only to defend our American past. If the creative minds that shaped our country were alive today they would doubtless be the first to tell us that we have no right to bank forever on their particular wisdom. The world does not stand still. Old wisdom may easily become new folly. They would tell us to gird up our courage and face the startlingly different world in which we now live. America, they would say, was not shaped once and for all in the days of its beginning. It was a dream of freedom that has to keep reshaping itself as new issues of life require new understanding and new efforts of will.

Primary to our psychological defense, therefore, must be an understanding of where we now are in the order of history, how we came to be where we now are, and where we are going from here.

## II

First, how we came to be where we now are. . . . The tragedy of our modern world goes deeper than events. It has its origin in a profound illogic. When we say this we are not saying a trifling thing, as if we were talking of some mere slip in an argument. Logic is of the very essence of our life. Take logic altogether out of our life and we are nothing at all. Logic is our human awareness of what follows from what.

If I put a match to dry paper, the paper will burn; if I drink poison—enough of it—I shall die; if I insult a man, I shall make him angry. "If this, then that";

endlessly repeated, this is the way the human mind works. Intelligence, quite simply, is a sense of what actually follows from what. Stupidity is continued error about what follows from what. Where there is no awareness whatever of what follows from what, we have an absence of all intelligence—idiocy or imbecility.

What has defeated us has been a successive breakdown in the logic of our life. We have not known, clearly and securely, what properly follows from what.

For a while—during past decades—a few linkages had seemed obvious to us. "If we work hard, if we plant and produce"—so we thought—"we shall build for ourselves and our children a secure prosperity." We did do this; and behold, the opposite happened. Our hardest work, our most plenteous production, turned into our present baffling economic disaster. Again, "If we encourage scientific research, we shall free ourselves from ancient drudgeries; we shall be a liberated human race." We did do this; and again note what happened. With the brilliant successes of science and invention came not only the enslavement of working populations, but—through poison gas, airplanes, high explosives, and the rest—such destruction and brutality as the world has never known. Again: "If (we Americans said) we honestly pursue among ourselves the ways of freedom, other peoples will follow, until freedom encircles the earth." We did pursue the ways of freedom—or thought we did—and today all over the world freedom has to fight for its life. Finally (worst of all our disappointments) we once said: "If we fight for democracy, we shall save democracy." We fought victoriously; but now, despite our victory, new tyrannies threaten to possess the world.

In all these cases we said: "If this, then that"; and in all these cases some mysterious reality beyond our knowledge replied: "If this, then assuredly *not* that."

Was it stupidity on our part that made us fail in our logic; or were we the victims of an unpredictability beyond anyone's knowing? It may indeed be that we are at one of those mutational points of history—one of those points of sudden leap—where even the best minds cannot know what the future has in store, and therefore what the future requires of them—like the point that marked the passage from feudalism to capitalism. If this is so, then we are exonerated from our several failures to sense the true "if this, then that." The failures, in that case, were merely those of individuals caught in a transitional stage of history. But before we take such comfort, we need to examine how our minds worked under the changing conditions of our world. Perhaps they did not work at all. Perhaps they merely drifted along in the same old way. Perhaps—

worst of all—they held on stubbornly to old habits of thought and action, when new habits were needed. It may be, in short, that at this change point of history our minds were not rightly intelligent.

## III

"If we work, if we plant and produce. . . ." The conclusion seemed inevitable. "*Of course*, if we work and produce, only excellent results will follow." And many of us—millions of us—bred in the tradition of energy and thrift, drew this conclusion. So we reasoned: "Let us freely go our energetic way; freedom of enterprise will win us prosperity." It had been a valid conclusion for centuries of human endeavor. But—and here was something that changed the logic—this century had brought strikingly new conditions. If the correct conclusion was now to be drawn, the "if" clause—"if we work, etc."—had to be more accurately stated. Conditions of work were now signally different from what they had ever been before. Almost overnight they had changed from laborious small-quantity production to easy huge-quantity production. Properly restated, then, the "if" clause should now have run: "If (with immensely increased productive power) we work, and plan, and produce. . . ."

This new entrant into the logic—"immensely increased productive power"—needed to be thought about. What would immensely increased productive power do to an economic setup? What would it require of us in the way of new economic arrangements? As the years of the economic depression have extended themselves far beyond expectation, we have been forced at last to think about this. And—dimly as yet—we begin to see a light. We begin to see that the great increase in the power to produce requires a proportionate increase in the power to purchase. To some of us this has become simple economic A B C. But this requires us to think further: many more things to sell need many more people to buy. The rich cannot absorb all the new things that can now be produced. Even if they could buy them—which they obviously cannot—they could not possibly use them. The logical conclusion, then, seems obvious: the new order requires that the masses of people become the customers of this new productive system.

This, too, is now simple economic A B C. But simple as it is in logic, it fails to pass over into action. Why? Because it makes a startling new demand upon us. It demands that we seek ways in which to increase the wealth of all the people. It demands, in short, that we find ways in which to make the *equal* rights to life, liberty, and the pursuit of happiness come true at last.

This, to most of us, is still too utterly foreign to contemplate. It means turning from our self-reliant absorption in our private affairs and giving heed to what the masses of people require. It means reconsidering the whole scheme of self-centered, competitive enterprise, where victories go to the few and defeats to the many. It means being willing to try for new arrangements that make for a widespread raising of the levels of life.

The logic is clear: modern production needs mass consumption. At last—after the terrors of crisis upon crisis—we begin to assent to this with our minds; but our wills still refuse to follow.

And so, because we are as yet convinced only with our brains, we are not yet prepared to do happily and intelligently what the logic of this new age demands of us. And because we will not follow the logic of our age, we still fail to create for that age a way for the secure enjoyment of what our human genius has made possible.

Obviously, then, the new age requires of us a rethinking of our total economic situation. Thus far we seem to have been unable to do this. We still stand reluctant before the future. Long habits of individualism keep us from enlisting wholeheartedly in efforts to raise the common level of life. The habits of a century and more of pioneering, of standing self-reliantly on our own feet, and of going about our own business, make it difficult for us to take over the concerns of low-income groups. We are still inclined to believe that if people do not have much, it is because they do not deserve much. We still believe that the race is to the swift and that God must take care of the stumbling ones. We carry, in short, the self-centered moralism of a simple rural society into the hugely complicated industrial society of today. We are not our brother's keeper—and we do not intend to be so.

But the logic of this new age requires a new moral outlook and habit of life. It is comparable to the vigorous assertion: "Either we all hang together or we all hang separately." Either the income level of all of us must be raised, or the income level of the fortunate few of us must be increasingly jeopardized. There can no longer be a small number of very rich and a vast number of very poor. Modern life, geared to mass production, must be geared likewise to mass fulfillment.

There is here a logic in our economic situation which we cannot possibly escape. Either we adjust our ways of life to this inevitable logic, or we shall continue in our confusions and defeats.

## IV

"If we encourage scientific research. . . ." Here again the conclusion seemed obvious. If truth is found, by the searchers after truth, what can possibly follow but good? Let the scientist in his laboratory devote himself to the search for what is true, and even though his discovery may be but one small fragment, that fragment will fit harmoniously into a total that is good.

It seemed excellent logic. It was the logic that animated the nineteenth and early twentieth centuries. But again—as we now look back on the brilliant discoveries of these centuries and note what has been done with them—we see that our "if this, then that" was oversimplified. We failed to note that a scientific discovery is not an isolated event that can be fitted neatly into a total mosaic of life. Every scientific discovery, and every technological application, alters the context of life. We have seen this happen in thousands of ways. The discovery of wireless communication has literally created a different world. It has enabled people to do things to people, and with people, in ways never possible before. To say that the discovery was a *truth* and therefore, as such, *good,* is to miss the fact that, fitted into a total context of life, it altered that context in all kinds of ways—good and also bad.

Our logic, then, should have run: "If we encourage scientific and technological research, *and if, as individuals and as a society, we take all precautions against possible evil uses of this research,* then we may confidently expect that good will follow." This, however, is precisely the logic we did not follow.

We may illustrate the illogic of our attitude by two

forms of evil: industrial and political. No one needs to be told that the triumphs of science and invention have wrought much havoc in the working life of people. To take one single example of an imminent evil: at the present moment we await the disaster that will come to thousands of workers when the cotton-picking machine is released for purchase. Thus far neither individuals nor society have found any way of so anticipating the disaster as to take steps to mitigate its full effect. The disaster will come; some of us will be sorry for the victims; but there will be no social obligation to restore them to the economic scheme of things. Obviously this is *laissez faire* at its worst, for here freedom to make and sell an invention is linked with an immense power to bring disaster to life.

One of the most significant signs of a dawning awareness of this illogic is the reluctance of the inventors of this new mechanism to place it on the market before adequate provision is made for the victims. The inventors refuse to believe that, since they have discovered a mechanical *truth*, what they have discovered is *ipso facto* good. They see—and should be honored for their seeing—that the mechanical truth they have discovered will be an evil unless it is fitted with intelligent justice into the going scheme of life. But thus far there are no indications that anyone in our society—lay or official—

knows how, or cares to discover how, to prepare for the mitigation of an apparently inevitable disaster.

Long ago H. G. Wells called our attention to this in his *Modern Utopia*, and suggested that a truly civilized society would take upon itself the obligation to re-educate and make new places for those displaced by new inventions. Wells's book was written in 1905. In this blessed year of Our Lord, society still washes its hands of the entire problem.

Our second illustration is from the field of politics. Daily, now, we have tragic reminders of the fact that perfectly good inventions—for example, airplanes and high explosives—have brought intolerable evil into the world of nations. The old *laissez-faire* logic that a nation has a right to fight for its rights by any means at its command has been maintained, even though what we call the "nation," equipped with these modern inventions, is a vastly different entity from what it was when there was no possibility of being so equipped. The power of the large modern "nation" to do evil has been so increased that it is literally no longer what it used to be, an association of people formed for the purpose of governing themselves; the nation is now potentially a mechanical monster, capable of a pitiless mastery never before possible. Since the high-powered "nation" of today is no longer the moderately powered nation of yesterday, the same reasoning cannot with accuracy be applied to it. New thinking has to be done. Can this modern potential monster be given free scope to work its will? Shall the new instruments of science be unrestrictedly at its command? When we cling to our traditional reasoning, holding that a nation today has the same right it always has had to fight as it pleases with any weapons it pleases, we commit the fallacy that logicians call "the fallacy of ambiguous middle." We use "nation" in two widely different senses.

Could we have properly forecast the increased power for international evil which new inventions would bring, we might have seen the need for some form of world-wide responsibility to prevent the disastrous uses to which they have been put. To an extent, we did forecast these evils. We talked of the possible destruction of civilization by the new mechanisms of war. But our traditional logic of *laissez faire* among nations, applied uncritically to the vastly more powerful nations of today, prevented our taking the steps a more adequate logic would have required. We continued, in short, to think about nations in old ways even while the new conditions demanded that we think about them in new ways. New weapons made necessary new obligations to control the use of those weapons. We needed to give up our *laissez-faire* ideas about what nations had the right to do. We needed to think in terms of the effects these high-powered nations could have upon the welfare of the world. We needed, in short, to think not in terms of single nations, but of nations all together. And so—tragically enough—our failure to establish a world-wide obligation for the control of the uses of science has turned science, unwittingly and unwillingly, into an enemy of mankind.

From examples such as these—in industry and politics—we are belatedly beginning to realize that science and invention are never isolated "goods." Science is what science does; invention is what invention does—in the hands of those who use them. Therefore, generously as we may accord to the scientist and technologist free scope for their investigations and inventions, the matter does not end there. Somehow and somewhere there will have to be responsibility for anticipating the uses to which science and invention are put, and for guarding against uses that are humanly disastrous.

Such responsibility scarcely exists today, either in industry or in government. And so it too frequently happens that the very triumphs of science become the graveyard of the race it serves. Science may indeed bring much incidental good; but without social aims and social controls, it inevitably brings much unnecessary evil. The logic of our age would seem to require that we equip ourselves with such social controls as will guarantee only the beneficent uses of science and technology.

This will not be an easy thing to do. When we have tried to do it in the past—as in attempts at pure food and drug acts—we have been opposed by selfish interests criminally determined to make wealth for themselves out of injury to others. Nevertheless, in spite of powerful opposition, we have to a degree succeeded in educating our minds to the need for such controls.

A similar beginning of awareness is found in the matter of armament control. As yet, little progress has been made, because old-fashioned thinking still maintains nations in their right to be unlimited in their choice of the mechanisms of destruction. International armament control waits on a convinced international-mindedness. The incredible tragedies of our time cry aloud for some unity of world conviction that will implement world control and take from nations the right to the irresponsible misuses of science.

However, much more will be needed than social con trols. Scientists who have a pride in their scientific integrity must learn to be actively furious at the misuses of their science. It will not be enough for them to be specialists in research; they must also be citizens sitting in judgment on the uses of their research. The chemist who discovers an ingenious way of adulterating foods may no longer excuse himself on the ground that as a *chemist* he is merely responsible for his chemical discovery. The psychologist who discovers ways in which behavior can be influenced through emotional appeals may likewise no longer excuse himself on the ground that as a *psychologist* he is merely responsible for his psychological discovery. Scientists and inventors have too easily rationalized their specialized irresponsibility. As scientists, however, they are obligated to be guardians of the science they are honored to serve. They have, therefore, to extend their minds beyond their specialized researches to the uses that are made of them. When they find that the uses are misuses, they as scientists are obligated to be vigorous and courageous in opposition.

What we need, therefore, is, first of all, social controls that guard us against the misuses of science. But we need, in the second place, scientists trained to think not only as scientists but also as citizens. Science must no longer be permitted to be a weapon to defeat the very humanity that brings it forth.

## V

One of our pleasant American illusions has been that if we mind our own business—and mind it well—things will turn out right. It may be doubted if we have ever learned to mind even our own business well. Minding our own business would have meant carrying out the objectives of our democracy: establishing liberty, equality, and justice in our midst, and making this a land where happiness may be genuinely pursued.

In theory this was what we were supposed to do. But we know that the practice has fallen far short of the theory. We were an energetic people, each one anxious to get ahead; and once having said, in our historic document, that we believed in liberty and equality, we proceeded to attend to our individual affairs, with the result that some of us did remarkably well, while most of us were reduced to the same old frustrated ways of life that had characterized the nondemocratic societies of history. Perhaps we were not quite so frustrated; but we were more so than a democratic society ought to have been happy about. Had we been able to become a shining example of a land of truly free men and women, a land of truly equal opportunities, there is no telling what this example might have meant to the rest of the world. The question is unanswerable, since the conditions were never fulfilled.

We are brought, then, to consider the peculiar illogic of our world outlook. This illogic has assumed a world of independent nations, each of which is supposed to have the right to carry on in ways that please it best. There has been the further assumption that each nation, minding its own business, would have no effect upon its neighbors.

Obviously this, again, has been false thinking—true, perhaps, in days of slow locomotion and communication, but no longer true when locomotion and communication became swift. Nowadays what one nation does—with its currency or tariffs or rattling of sabers or dumpings on the market—inevitably affects other nations. There is not today, nor has there been for a half-dozen decades, any national independency in all the world. There is instead the most intricate and delicate interdependence.

With our left hand we have recognized this interdependence. We have made treaties, formed alliances, issued politely worded diplomatic reprimands, extended favors or withheld them. We have acted as if we had to take careful and continuous notice of other nations, adjust our conduct to theirs, and hope that their conduct would be adjusted to ours. With the left-hand side of our minds we have built a network of relationships which may some day become the texture of a new world society.

But with our right hand we have sworn allegiance to sovereign independence; and with the right-hand side of our mind we have repudiated all efforts to implement interdependence with a world organization adequate to what our interrelationships require. Like Hamlet, we have continued to stand irresolute before the act of decision: to be the united world we needed to be, or to be the fragmented world of jealous nations we ought no longer to be but could not bring ourselves not to be.

Every realistic factor in today's world urges us forward to some form of union, while every sentimental factor—of memory, tradition, local patriotism, familiarity—pulls us back to the old, ineffective fragmentation.

It is not an easy question for us to settle; but the logic of contemporary events would seem to point to some form of interrelationship closer and more effectively implemented than exists today.

The tragedy of our times would here again seem to arise out of logical obtuseness. "If this, then that. . . ." If the world today is close-drawn by swift locomotion, swift communication, and by economic and cultural interdependence, then assuredly it must be consciously and vigorously geared to such interrelationships. We cannot at once be interdependent and at the same time neglect to fashion the world organization that interdependence requires. To be interdependent and act as if we were independent is to live a contradiction. Obviously, it is this contradiction we live today. Good citizens and true, we are—most of us—horrified at the mere suggestion of a departure from ancestral ways. Fired with nationalistic loyalty, we push aside the logic of the contemporary world and require that the older logic of a fragmented world be maintained. Because we demand an older logic in a world where innumerable linkages require a new one, we keep on failing. We substitute the illusory freedom of independence for the more difficult but solider freedom of interdependence.

This is an easy thing, of course, for me as an individual to say. I am accusing my fellow Americans. I am making it plain that I think they ought to have been better thinkers. Heaven keep me from such presumption! I have been a pretty poor thinker myself—a poor thinker because I have thought only with the surface of my mind and with very little of my will. I have done practically nothing to advance the cause of world union. I have believed in it; but pleasantly, unobtrusively, in the manner of sitting in front of a fireplace and talking it over with friends. I have talked of world union as a far vision. I have not really expected it to be achieved—at least, not in my lifetime. And so, in point of fact, I have joined with my fellow Americans in believing that, matters being as they are, the best thing we could do was to mind our own affairs. The only credit I can give myself is that I have been insistent that we mind them well.

What I need—what we all need now—is to bring our world-union ideas out of the region of mild theoretical assent into the region of practical intent. We need here and now to discover ways of advancing ourselves toward world union. This is not easy, for most of us have no way of impressing the heads of nations or the citizens of nations with the idea that they ought to contrive a new relationship between themselves. We can, indeed, preach the gospel of world union. But the details of such a union are still uncertain. Besides, the status of all the nations of the world is so precarious that any proposal for a present union rests on shifting sands.

The depths of our present difficulty are made vivid by the fact that we, as sincere believers in a new relationship between nations, can as yet find no practical way of helping toward such relationships. Perfectly well aware, as we are, that if nations go on in their present irresponsible separateness no fruitful order of life can be hoped for, we seem, nevertheless, unable as individuals to advance the cause of a rational world order.

Yet the matter is not as hopeless as it might appear to be. We can hearten ourselves by recalling that every new invention has behind it a long struggle to get the clear idea. Clear ideas are not easy to get. Inventors search and fret and fume—and still the idea eludes them. The idea—once it is caught—becomes the powerful, creative thing.

In the world of nations we need a new invention. But first we need the clear, creative idea. We thought we had it when we formed the League of Nations. Perhaps there was a fragment of the inventive idea in that. But something more seems needed now.

Inventive ideas do not come—or seldom come—like bolts out of the blue. They come by fumbling, by trying this and that, by exploring, formulating, and rejecting. They come by effort.

Here is something for our bewildered minds to do. We can cease being lackadaisical about this crucial need of our times, and can make it our business to think hard and persistently, critically and tough-mindedly, about what a united order of life may properly be. We have no right to push the issue aside as none of our business, nor may we any longer make the matter merely one of pleasant discussion. Because we want a less cruel and disastrous world, because we want such a world for our children and their children, this problem of a new order for the world is our most pressing business.

## VI

America began as a new adventure in human association. It must continue as an adventure. The worst defense of ourselves would be a call to defend merely what we have thus far achieved.

To be strongly American, we need to be glad of the chance that this turn of history gives us to help create the kind of civilization that has never yet been fully shaped into being. To do this we have to do new thinking. We have to come to terms with the mistakes we have made, and, even at the cost of giving up old familiar labels, move toward a more intelligent grasp of what this new order of life requires of us.

The poet Robinson called us

> . . . an inflexible and hasty nation
> That sees already done
> Rather too much that has not yet begun.[1]

In the face of the grave dangers that now threaten us, we have to come down from our high-horse Americanism, from our belief that we are the "best ever." We have to achieve a new humility—of self-criticism and redirected effort of will.

[1] E. A. Robinson, "Dionysus in Doubt," *Collected Works* (New York: Macmillan & Co.), p. 860.

# TOWARD A BEGINNING

## I

If the foregoing analysis is correct, we of our age have failed in our logic. The age has required something of us, but we have been unable to see what it required. So —to repeat the words of the litany—we have done the things we ought not to have done and have left undone the things we ought to have done.

No doubt, this logical failure of ours goes deeper than our intellects. It goes down into our feelings and habit-systems. The Hebrew writer expressed it thus: "As a man thinketh in his heart so is he." Thinking in one's heart is different from thinking merely with one's head. Our failure in logic, in short, has in reality been a failure in our basic feeling and will about life. We have not been able to think effectively about what the age requires of us because we have not yet learned to care about things and people as this new age requires us to care.

In all we have said, it is obvious that the new conditions of life require a feeling and will on our part that are more than self-centered. They require a habit of mind that takes in others. Even from the most self-interested point of view this is so. The producer, now, has to think of the consumer; the seller of the buyer. He cannot any longer say "The public be damned" and get away with it. If the public is really damned, he himself is damned. In other words he has to care about whether people are able to buy things and enjoy them even though he himself does not care a rap for these same people.

This is indeed a fairly low level of caring about others; but it is at least a beginning. It at least causes the aforesaid producer or seller to care whether the income level of people is sufficiently high for them to buy his goods. If it is not sufficiently high, if his goods go begging in a market where people stand with empty pockets, he will be likely to bestir himself. He will begin to lend an ear to proposals for increasing the purchasing power of people. He may even do something about it himself.

This is precisely the way the thing worked with the officials of one of our great mail-order houses. They discovered that the farmers in a certain backward region of the South were too poverty-stricken to buy the goods they offered for sale. They did not thereupon damn them as poor white trash, lazy and inefficient. They deliberately thought out ways in which they could help these money-poor farmers to increase their income. First of all they tackled the problem of their health. These farmers, they saw, living on their pork and corn-pone diet, were simply too weak in body to make a decent living out of their land. So they sent down a man to teach them how to raise vegetables to add to their diet. The thing worked. Not only were the farmers, however, helped to a more wholesome diet; they learned, through their gardening, ways in which to increase their income. The upshot of it was better living for the farmers—and new customers for the mail-order house.

It is a simple idea to get hold of—that what is good for people is inevitably good for business. This is precisely the idea that businessmen of the past few decades have not had. They have felt no responsibility beyond accumulating as much profit as they could for themselves. They have understood their philosophy of free enterprise to mean "Get as much as you can for yourself and there will be prosperity for all." They need now to revise this to read: "Get as much as you legitimately can for yourself by helping others to get as much as they legitimately can for themselves, and there will be prosperity for all." A recent writer has rephrased the old self-interest philosophy thus: "In a modern democracy . . . the protection of exigent self-interests proceeds simultaneously with a necessary and intelligent solicitude for the like interests of others." [1]

This is not social-mindedness at its highest level, but it is the level we shall have first to achieve before we can hope to reach one that is higher. There is a tendency among some people who see the devastation wrought by a too self-centered philosophy of business enterprise to urge that what we now need is a moral and religious transformation of men—a sheer change in them from self-interest to that love of mankind which sinks the interests of self in the interests of others. Doubtless something like this must eventually be achieved, but it is folly to expect that it can be achieved at once. Even the best of us are still, in the main, creatures of self-interest. What avails most today is to make our self-interest intelligent. An intelligent self-interest takes in the interests of others. If we could get this type of self-interest going widely in our economic society today we should begin to move rapidly toward the socialization of life. Then, as we increasingly grew the habit of including the interests of others in our considerations, we should gradually build the habit of *liking* to include the interests of others. This is the way the social mind is developed. It is a matter of the gradual

[1] Ordway Tead, *New Adventures in Democracy* (New York: Whittlesey House), p. 145.

·wth of the habit of thinking of what is good for ·rs.

'hen, at last, we *like* to think about the good of ·s, and do so continuously and warmly, we shall reached the worthier ethical level. But this doubt- is still—save in the case of a few exceptional indi- ·iduals—a long way off. It would be enough if we could at least achieve this basic outlook: "*My* welfare requires *your* welfare." What has brought economic and other disaster—here in America and all over the world —is that even this small amount of socialized outlook has as yet not been widely achieved. We are still largely at the stage of "*My* welfare is my own concern."

## II

For a long time now we have been witness to a long knockdown and drag-out fight between employers and workers. The fight ought never to have begun, for if employers had been halfway decent it would never have been necessary. It began at a time—in the early nineteenth century—when business did not need workers as customers. It could regard them as negligible riffraff. Business, with its slow methods of production, had all it could do to supply the "gentry." Hence, with brutal unconcern, employers kept workers at the lowest level at which they could manage to survive.

It is not a pretty story. Businessmen who read of the barbarities committed in mines, shops, and factories—barbarities done to women and children as well as to men—have cause to blush at the inhumanity that their business forerunners visited upon their fellows.

Those times are now past, but the spirit of them is not wholly absent from business and industry. There are still economic overlords who insist upon retaining the power to grind the faces of their workers, to keep their wages down and their rights as human beings unrecognized. But these men are merely the last of a dying race.

Business now needs the worker—as a customer. Alert employers know this and want their workers to be well paid and self-respecting. For business, they know, is better in a community of well-paid, well-fed, well-clothed, and self-respecting workers than in a community of underpaid, half-starved, humiliated, and spiritless wage slaves.

I remember hearing a business executive say, over twenty years ago, "We have set for ourselves a new policy: we believe in more profits for ourselves and more pay for our workers." Those were days in which the average businessman went about growling that profits could be increased only by cutting wages. This business executive was the forerunner of a type of executive that has come to stay.

Workers are customers. Business injures itself to the extent that it keeps its customers poor. But workers are also human beings who make the psychological responses that human beings are accustomed to make. The matter of a better wage is not merely one of being able to buy more things. It is, more deeply, a matter of added self-respect. Added self-respect means more energizing; more energizing means more competence, which means better workmanship.

So the circle goes round. What is good for the worker turns out to be good for business. And what is genuinely good for business turns out to be good for the worker. The way of economic mutualism is the wise way of economic life.

Here, then, is the beginning of a new attitude that will eventually lead to a more humanized relation between employer and employee. Hitherto that relation has been largely one between enemies. It has already advanced beyond that. Where employers freely recognize the right of their employees to organize in their own defense and to bargain collectively, the relationship has advanced to one between friendly enemies. Employers who have reached this stage of relationship are learning increasingly to like it. They prefer to bargain with self-respecting workers organized in, and standing on, their own right rather than to continue the old method of browbeating sullen and resentful underlings. Employers are learning that there can be a pleasure in mutual respect that is far greater than the pleasure of unmitigated power.

We may look forward to another advance—where employers are as interested in the welfare of their workers as they are in their own profits. Some employers have reached this stage. More of them will reach it as the new habit grows of according to workers the right of a decent standard of wage and security.

## III

In the past few years a new conception of the attitude of government toward its distressed citizens has taken shape among us. It is one of the mild revolutions that is part of the larger revolution now sweeping the world.

Americans will remember President Hoover's sad blunder in relation to the army of unemployed in Washington. It was the last expression that we shall probably ever witness of the old attitude that a man's private distresses are his private affairs, with which government need have no concern. Hoover swept the miserable army of unemployed Americans out of Washington, but he swept them into the conscience of America. There will never be need of another march on Washington. The American nation now goes to the unemployed citizen in his own community and gives him aid.

There are a few cynical folk who, in their comfortable clubs, denounce this as a new debauching of the manhood and womanhood of America—they themselves being the still honorably undebauched! But by and large the giving of relief to those who have in no wise been to blame for their misfortunes has now become an accepted and approved habit of the American people. The reason is a twofold one: (1) Americans do not enjoy seeing millions of their fellow Americans suffer; (2) They cannot *afford* to let them suffer.

It would seem ungracious to say that the second is the more potent reason; and yet it must be remembered that in earlier crises, time after time, millions of people throughout the land were permitted to go unhelped save in such small ways as private citizens could devise. Americans then were not averse to witnessing suffering in their midst. What has brought about the difference?

The answer would seem to lie in the statement so often repeated of late, that business itself cannot recover unless the purchasing power of these millions of unemployed is maintained. These unemployed were *customers*. Government must see to it that they still remain customers.

Again it is a simple case of mutualism. We can no longer—*for our own sake*—afford to let vast numbers of our citizens be denied the power to purchase. And so we Americans adopt a new governmental attitude of relief, one that doubtless will never be reversed.

Does this sound too starkly selfish? But we are building a new habit in ourselves, the habit of doing something about the unfortunate in our midst. As yet the habit roots in little more than economic expediency; but we are learning to like what we are doing. We are preferring to give even the little that we give to seeing our fellow men desperate with need. Gradually the liking to help will become stronger in us than the will to economic expediency. Eventually we shall adopt as a national policy the fact that widespread economic distress among our people is a matter for instant governmental concern. Unconsciously, then, we are advancing from our philosophy of "each for himself" to the democratic philosophy of "all for each."

This advance toward a more democratic concern for our fellow citizens is evidenced likewise by the governmental shouldering of problems that have arisen out of our past mistakes. The tragedy of the Dust Bowl called forth the engineering energies of the nation. Here, too, it is a matter of good business. If the Dust Bowl grows worse, we shall grow worse with it. Nevertheless, this is something new in our American history—

that we undertake not only the reclaiming of lost lands but the rehabilitation of lost people.

We have only just begun to move in this new direction of a national concern for our fellow Americans. Sharecroppers and migratory workers, cotton pickers in the South, underpaid workers throughout the nation —these all need our attention. Our *laissez-faire* philosophy still keeps us from making efforts to better their condition. But a new habit is forming in us of concern for those who blamelessly are in distress. In no long distant time we Americans may awaken fully to the democratic obligation of guaranteeing to all the rights to life, liberty, and the pursuit of happiness.

Thus, in a number of ways, we are beginning to correct the mistakes in our logic. We are developing a sense of the interrelatedness of the interests of all our people. We are still too deeply committed to the individualistic philosophy of our economic life to make this sense of interrelatedness count greatly toward the reorganization of business and governmental life. We are not likely to become a fully socialized nation overnight. But the starkness of our individual self-concern is already a thing of the past. We are beginning, in small but significant ways, to learn that we are members one of another. The hope is that the learning will go on.

★ *9* ★

# THE EVIL THAT GOOD PEOPLE DO

## I

WHEN millions of honest people are dead set against doing things in the ways they now need to be done, something is bound to crack. Today the world is cracking all around us. Only incidentally is this happening because there are villains on the loose. Basically it is happening because millions of us "good people" have not yet learned to be good enough. Our spirits are willing but our minds are muddled.

When we were in the midst of the insanity of the first World War, it seemed the most natural thing in the world that we should make such insanity no longer possible. For a time it seemed as if we were to succeed. All around us people were saying: "This thing must not happen again. Nations cannot be allowed to go on the rampage. They must be made to give up their sovereign right to do as they please." It looked as if we were then and there to take the next great step in history—from nationalism to world commonwealth.

Then the psychological moment passed. The war was over. We were back on our jobs. Familiar things looked good again. Insensibly, we forgot the passion of our resolution to build a new world in which war should have no place. Other nations of the world, to be sure, made an effort to carry out the resolution by creating a League of Nations. We ourselves, contracted to the compass of our beloved America, would have nothing of it. America looked good enough to us. We yawned in the face of the world.

We were good people, but not good enough. Our minds refused to move out of their familiar grooves. We had been born Americans and Americans we proposed to remain.

This is our tragedy, that, confronted by a deep and resistless necessity, we were unable to adjust our minds to its requirements. Imperialistic nationalism had bred a chaos of competing jealousies and aggressivenesses. The time was more than due for a world overhauling. When we were asked to join in the reconstruction, we pulled out our traditional formula of "no entangling alliances" and told the world we were not interested.

It is easiest to blame evil people for our troubles.

Conspicuously evil people are fewer than good. It is therefore easier to discover them and do something about them. Thus, in the first World War, it seemed enough for us to repeat that the Kaiser had brought on the war. "Hang the Kaiser!" As simple as that! In those days very few individuals were sufficiently informed to know that it was common, ordinary people in all the belligerent countries, and their out-of-the-ordinary diplomatic representatives, who had set the stage and prepared the plot for the world tragedy; that it was merchants and manufacturers, bankers, college professors, editorial writers, lawyers, and ambassadors who, naïvely identifying national greatness with economic expansion, had pushed their nations to the point where they made truculent demands, rattled their sabers, and talked big about honor and destiny.

It is the good people—not the conspicuously bad—who invariably do most damage. For good people are legion. They set the pace and establish the tone of a society. Their intentions are excellent; but when their minds are geared to wrong ideas, they have a way of going forth in all innocence and earnestly doing the things that precisely ought not to be done.

Edwin Arlington Robinson pays his respects to such ill-informed, massed goodness:

> . . . if a drowsy wisdom blinks and leans
> Too much on legioned innocence

Armed only with a huge mistake,
Something is due to shake.[1]

In all kinds of ways, during the past few decades, we in America—we need not now speak of the rest of the world—have been "armed only with a huge mistake." We needed to pass beyond imperialistic nationalism; but we mistakenly believed that the nation—particularly our nation—was the crowning work of man. We needed to pass beyond the making of ever-deadlier weapons of war. But not even the exposure of the cynical practices of the armament ring could stir us into a passionate demand that our armament conferences do a thorough job. Private business felt uneasy about government intervention, even in a grave matter like this; and we, who had no shares in Steel, felt uneasy about being hard on private business. So we let private business retain its right to arm the countries that would in time force us to rearm. We hated war, yet—in all innocence—we allowed the continuance of the very conditions that made war an inevitable part of the world picture.

We needed to pass beyond the kind of business enterprise that plunged the masses of our citizenry into poverty and near poverty; beyond the kind of business that was even plunging itself into a major crisis. Yet we held with virtuous stubbornness to "rugged individ-

[1] E. A. Robinson, "Dionysus in Doubt," *Collected Works* (New York: Macmillan & Co.), p. 866.

ualism." When the Great Depression came, we grew frightened, and for a time we seemed at the point of sending our creaking economic system to the shops for repair. But when we had passed beyond the worst of the crisis–when we had reopened our banks and converted the millions of still-unemployed into a submissive army of subsidized reliefers–we insisted that the old mechanism be run as usual. Those who were mildly persistent in their efforts to remodel the economic machine were denounced as "revolutionary," as heading us toward "collectivism"–or toward any other ism we hated. Any thought that the twentieth century was different from the eighteenth and needed a twentieth-century economic equipment was beyond the comprehension of millions of us.

Our minds, in short, simply refused to function. Having been shaped to old expectations, we simply went on expecting the old things. Even as tragedy deepened in our own country and throughout the world, we continued to do business at the old stand. Millionaires kept on being made in the same old hearty fashion. Millions of people kept on scrabbling for a poor livelihood in the same old accepted way. There seemed to be no power in us to take our minds in hand, to forget our traditional absorptions long enough to do a job of economic reconstruction and human rehabilitation.

Anyone who is familiar with conditions in Germany after the war knows that Hitlerism was born out of the desperation of half-starving people. Anyone who is familiar with France and England during the era of appeasement knows that the support of Hitler was born out of a fear among the "good" business people that the old order of privilege might be overturned by the Communists. The unparalleled tragedy of today, with its threat to all the things we care about, was wrought by the good people—poor as well as rich—whose minds could not compass the thought that the new age requires a more humanized economics and a more responsible international setup.

## II

And here is the irony of this tragedy that has come upon us: *a totalitarian dictatorship is now doing in monstrous ways many of the things we ought to have been doing in intelligent ways.* We fumbled the job and the gangsters took it over.

Thus totalitarianism is wiping out national boundaries. It is taking from nations the right to exist independently and bringing them within the unity of a projected larger whole. It is doing this, however, by bloodshed and terror, by humiliation and enslavement. It is seeking to force upon Europe and Asia a unity that should have been wrought voluntarily and rationally, without injuring self-respect, and with enhanced freedom of individuals and groups.

Again, totalitarianism is swinging all individuals—young and old—into the service of the larger whole to which they belong. But it is doing this by drastic compulsion and by the fanatic falsification of values. The new age does, indeed, require the socializing of individuals, for democratic freedom can no longer go hand-in-hand with individual irresponsibility and unconcern. But the new age requires that the socializing be done through an educative process—through a change that takes place inside of people, voluntarily and without lies.

Finally, totalitarianism enlists all enterprises—business, professional, scientific, cultural—in the service of the larger whole. It recognizes no *laissez faire*—no freedom of business or profession or science or art—to do as it pleases, but it does its enlisting by compulsion; it regiments and administers. In so doing it has gained enormous power for itself. It has been able to weld national resources into a unity so powerful that it is a terror to the world. The new age likewise requires the unification of all enterprises in the service of the common welfare, but it requires that such unification be achieved through freedom.

Totalitarianism is a Frankenstein monster. It looks

like the real thing, but it lacks the essence that is life. It links nations together; it sweeps individuals and enterprises into the service of a larger whole; but it does all this with the clank of mechanical exactitude. The unity and socializing we seek in our new age must come out of an understanding that is free. Only free people with free minds can build a world that is good enough to live in.

There is a dangerous tendency among some people to believe that since the totalitarians are doing all these things that have long needed to be done, they are on the "wave of the future." There could be no profounder, no more tragic error. The "wave of the future"—if by that we mean the logical necessities of our age—is indeed carrying us toward a wider and deeper humanization of life. Many of us have tried to push back that wave, to disregard the logical necessities, to hold to "rugged individualism" and "no entangling alliances." Inevitably, we shall have to stop being futile. Inevitably, as the user of this phrase so finely says, we shall have to ride the wave into a more decent future. But the totalitarians are not on this wave. They seem to be accomplishing the *ends* we should all desire, but the means they use—and the philosophy underlying those means—are in direct contradiction to the ends. An enslaved world, however unified, is not the world called for by the logic of our times. A frenzied populace, cheering lies and rushing forth to beat up helpless people, is not the socialized populace for which our logic calls.

It would be the most tragic pity of all history if good people were to commit this last, incredible blunder, of supposing that, through the gangsterism of dictatorship, we were actually moving toward the acceptable future.

Totalitarianism is a powerful monster that clanks its way toward the overlordship of the world. Free people do ill to stand at the curb and feebly cheer it on. The task of free people is to make their free minds come alive. The old ways will no longer do. We have to find new ways. *We* have to find them—not the dictators.

# * *10* *

# FINDING AVENUES TO ACTION

## I

EUROPE brought to our attention a psychological truth: people can be induced to do anything if given a sense of importance. No one would have believed that civilized individuals could be inspired to do the incredibly bestial things that German Storm Troopers have done. It is said in psychological quarters that you cannot induce a man under hypnosis to do murder. But give him a sense of importance, and, in full awareness, he will even do murder.

It would be easy for us to dispose of this, as some people do, by saying that Germany is just a nation of hoodlums. That answer is too easy. In the first place, we all remember a Germany that was not a nation of hoodlums; in the second place, we have only to look around in our own country to see that hoodlumism is not confined to Europe. Name-calling may be a way of avoiding a problem, but it is never a way of solving one. When whole crowds of people within a world that thought itself civilized turn almost eagerly to the doing of uncivilized things, it is probably wiser to ask what the social pattern did not satisfy in those people than simply to assume that they are different from the truly civilized rest of us. This may help us, in the present crisis, to see grave defects in our own social pattern, defects that we need quickly to correct if we are not to go in similar ways.

Long ago, Tom Paine said, in another American crisis, "These are times to try men's souls." We might say now that these are times to check up on what kinds of souls we have been making.

## II

Our tradition is, in a sense, a curiously double one. We have tried to tell people to look after themselves, and at the same time to look after other people—that is, to be voluntarily and simultaneously self-interested and socially generous. I am not saying that the combination is impossible. All of us who really believe in democracy must believe that it is possible to work our way toward a condition in which people realize that their long-range self-interest is identical with the long-range common good. Indeed, we have staked our democratic hopes on coming to the stage where what is good for society is voluntarily accepted by us as good for each and every one of us. Unfortunately, we have not yet reached this stage. Social generosity still lags far behind. It is important for us to ask why this is so.

Think again of that twofold tradition—self-interest and social generosity. Neither can be expressed in a vacuum. Both have to be expressed in concrete situations. But what are the situations that our society has deliberately provided, and how well designed have these been to give people an equal skill in self-interest and social generosity? The simple fact is that we have deliberately trained people to be skillful in self-interest, while we have left more or less to accident their chance to find practical ways of being socially generous.

Self-interest has been continuously fortified in our people by two things: first, by the stark need to survive; second, by an education that has served chiefly as an introduction to the past and as a means of earning a living. It has never yet conceived itself as a schooling in applied generosity.

Take, first of all, the stark need to survive. We have, indeed, moved far from the primitive level of fear where every man's hand was against every other man's, and where the one constant, absorbing interest was that of managing to stay alive. But we have barely begun to reach the stage where we give people the slightest assurance that their society cares a rap about them if they are unable, in the competitive system, independently to make the grade. Not only the survival of the body, but that of self-respect has been tied with a tight knot to the self-interested effort to find a job, hold a job, get a raise, know the right people, live in the right community, put by something against a rainy day, and all the rest.

We have, then, the terrifying phenomenon of both the animal urge to survive and the psychological urge to be a personality lined up with self-interest. In practical terms this has meant that generosity has been given its outlet only in skimpy and haphazard fashion. The amazing phenomenon is that the impulse to be socially generous has so persistently survived in spite of everything. Even in our anxiously competitive world people do give to help other people; but they give a pittance, because they have never had enough freedom from worry to risk giving more. Too often social generosity, like recreation, has been something people have felt they could postpone until they got life well in hand; until they had made a security for themselves. But most people in our society have never achieved security—just as most have never achieved a voluntary retirement; and those who have achieved it have found their powers of social generosity as awkwardly untrained as their powers of self-entertainment.

If a will to help people and to contribute to the common good is to be our chief leaven against the effect of a concentrated self-interest, then that voluntary generosity has to be more than a kind of incidental which can always be left out if practical necessity demands. It has to be deliberately provided for in the scheme of our society.

## III

Let us consider this further fact—that we have not, in our educational system, trained individuals to be skillful in either personal generosity or communal effort. On the playing field, to be sure, or in the Boy Scouts or Campfire Girls, we provide a school-age opportunity for converting the abstract ideal of good sportsmanship into concrete behavior. We deliberately provide ways by which individuals can increase their self-respect by serving something larger than themselves. But we make no such concrete provision for post-school generosity.

Does any school in America deliberately plan specific outlets for generosity? Does any school focus the attention of growing youngsters upon the various avenues which, when they are adults, they may follow in order to become happily and effectively a part of the mutual-aid side of life?

What almost invariably happens—and this is one of the saddest tragedies of our society—is that we turn youngsters out into a world that takes from them most of the fellowship-situations they have enjoyed in school without welcoming them into new fellowship-situations.

Think what happens to an average young man when the doors of school or college finally close behind him. He has been part of a student group; he has been, perhaps, part of a team; he has worked on the school paper; he has probably been in a school play; he has tooted his special toot in the school band—and that toot was necessary and important not in itself, but because it contributed to a whole. Suddenly he is an adult. Now what is he supposed to do? Where is the situation in which he can continue any one of the group skills he has learned? If he toots his toot now, there is no band either to support it or to need it. Now he is suddenly told that he had better get to work and make a living. Now it is up to him to see to it that he can support a wife and family. In the tense effort to get what he needs, he is alone. Even his former teammates—even the former members of that band—are converted from helpers into competitors. He goes to work if he can find work to do. If he is among the "lucky" who can keep a job for many years, he may eventually be awarded a dinner and a watch by the company for which he works.

His hair is a little thin by this time, and the dreams of school or college are wistful dreams to be recalled on alumni day. They are not half so vivid as the present need for getting together enough money to keep the insurance from lapsing and making the monthly payments on the suburban house that stands in a line with other fairly identical suburban houses.

What, during the twenty years or so, has become of his sense of good sportsmanship, his love of teamwork, his honest wish to be of use? Good sportsmanship, too often, is something that he experiences vividly only when he goes to a world series game or sits in a crowd at a boxing match. There he is as quick as ever to resent a foul. Intellectuals who delight in making fun of the average American's interest in sports where he is merely an onlooker seem not to have come to grips with the fact that even as an onlooker he enjoys a continuity with his boyhood ideal of being a good sport. But from the game he goes back into the office or the bank or the store. And he is "not in business for his health." There, in that business world, he is in an area where the need to survive has produced an accepted system of compromises.

What other outlet does he have for his wish to be

not too starkly alone in the human venture? He can join a lodge or a service club; but over the activities of these, as over those of the baseball diamond and the boxing ring, there hangs a curious air of nostalgia. He can, indeed, be as much one of the crowd as he was in school. But he cannot often move beyond this to a fully mature type of self-giving through group endeavor. For no sooner does the group push itself beyond the obvious surface techniques of unity than it comes up against an economic system in which there is the need of all the individual members to survive and competitively prosper.

It is much the same thing with women in their groups. They can, and do, work for "causes." But these causes themselves have to be fairly innocuous. Service clubs and women's clubs have made a large and generous contribution to help for the helpless. They have supported boys' and girls' clubs, helped orphanages, raised donations for a myriad good causes. That they have done so seems unanswerable evidence that people want to be kind even when the chances to be kind are largely against them.

But always, just back of their confident surface efforts to help, is a caution, an unacknowledged awareness that there are sufferings too great to be faced if their way of doing things is to be a source of pride to them. They can tinker a little with incidents of suffering; they cannot examine the mechanism of society that gives them their own power to survive.

No one with any psychological discernment would say that the men and women of our middle class are radiantly happy people. They are too constantly torn between their will to be secure and their will to be socially generous.

There are, of course, in our society numerous organizations that are trying to come to grips with social problems. These range from the help-giving to the socially reconstructive groups. Often the people in these groups are animated by a great sincerity and by a genuine will to work out of our atomic society into one of mutual aid. But the setup of our life is such that even these best of groups get no more than a niggardly chance to enjoy a sense of social unity and common faith. These, like the other groups of which we have spoken, are brought up sharply against the economic system. The chief difference is that they know the system is there as a thing to be reckoned with. Too often, in order to accomplish anything at all, they are turned into groups that are *against* other groups. In them the will to overcome and the techniques of overcoming are more consistently cultivated than are the habits of full-rounded mutuality.

It is not a happy picture. And yet, in a sense, it is an encouraging one. It is encouraging because the generosities among us refuse to be atrophied even by the most intense need to think about ourselves. Even our haphazard, incidental will to be socially generous fills the coffers of our community chests, of our Red Cross, of our community hospitals. It provides group life for thousands upon thousands of young people. It stands as a last bulwark between those who fail and starvation.

Deviously and tenaciously it stays alive. When a crisis comes, whether it be a flood, an earthquake, or a war, the will to give, the will to yield ourselves to something greater than ourselves, surges up with an onrush that refuses to be confined within the puny channels of ordinary giving. Thus the spirit of man calls for a chance to give itself. But all too often, save in times of crisis, it finds no channel open to it, no ways prepared in which it can make good its will to set the common interest above self-interest.

## IV

It is war crisis that puts the severest test to our untrained will to generosity. War crisis often does a curious thing to people: it calls for their most intense efforts in the service of the larger good; but all too often it turns these efforts into activities that work to destroy the larger good.

It is a well-known fact in psychology that when a strong impulse can find no normal, wholesome outlet, it is likely to find a perverted one. When a myriad people who have not learned to be skilled in ways of social helpfulness wish, in wartime, to be helpful, what they are most likely to do is the simple, direct, primitive thing of hating. Since they cannot hate in general, they proceed to hate in particular. And since hating an enemy in a distant land, however necessary, is at best only a futile indulgence, they proceed to look for enemies within their own land that they can not only hate, but hate effectively.

This is the psychological situation that we are now beginning to confront. It involves a profound danger, but also an opportunity.

We face peril not only from what antidemocrats in our midst will do, but from what our own sincere, democratic-minded people will do. The latter peril lies in the fact that, in many cases, these people will be unable to distinguish between the real enemies in our midst and those who are merely enough unlike themselves to be exciting objects of hate. What is so threatening in the present situation is the fact that the real enemies among us are incredibly adroit in appearing to be exactly like ourselves. They have no scruples that prevent their mouthing our American phrases and declaring their loyalty to American tradition. They will do and say anything to forward their effort to bore from within.

It is those who have scruples, who persist in making distinctions between good and bad even within our own country, who are likely to be caught in the web of hatred. Again, it is those who suffer the handicap of a different colored skin or a different accent. Those who are either the distinctive individuals who might create a better society or those who are meekly unaware of what the whole thing is about are likely to be the ones who stand out as different, and as therefore the most tempting objects of wrath. It will not be those who are devilishly clever at being different in soul but identical in words and appearance.

This is one of our chief dangers today. It is very real. But the opportunity born of crisis is no less real. Now, if ever, is our chance to do what we have failed to do in the past; namely, to take seriously people's wish to be of use, their intense desire to be important not only as competitive individuals but as part of a larger whole to which they can contribute. Now is the chance to give release to the generous impulses of our people by creating concrete situations in which their generosity can be exercised.

We shall need, in a time of war crisis, to find generous and constructive things for our people to do lest in all innocence and sincerity they find for themselves cruel and destructive things to do. If we can do this, we shall be laying the foundation for a post-crisis expertness in social generosity. The important thing now is not to do things that will have to be psychologically undone when the crisis is over. Rather we need to do things that both serve the cause of national defense now and the cause of democracy hereafter.

## V

A nation that defends itself has to do more than prepare an army; it has also to prepare its people. One thing it has to do is to raise the health levels of its people where these are low, for poor vitality cannot create strong morale. This means that there must be better food, better housing, better chances for recreation, better conditions for work. Here is a chance for patriotic service. Who are better equipped than the happily-circumstanced to work with experts in the public health field?

Another thing a nation has to do is to give what has been called "catastrophe education." English people of all classes have undergone such education. They know what to do when the siren blows; how to carry a wounded person to shelter; how to give first aid; how to take care of children; how to distribute food and clothing. American preparation for defense must include such education of its citizens. Here again is patriotic service that can absorb the energies of a person. During the last war many a wealthy girl got her first satisfied sense of service, as well as her sense of genuine importance, by driving an ambulance on the battlefields of France. We need not wait for war to invade our land. Even now we can organize catastrophe education throughout the country and enlist men and women to be the lay teachers of their fellows.

Another thing a nation has to do is to so vitalize the recreational life of its people that they get the feeling of belonging together. In times of peace we drift into separateness. We go to our entertainments as isolated individuals and come away as isolated individuals. There will be the need to quicken the sense of being a united people. Here, again, is a chance for patriotic service. Many an individual can be induced to go full steam ahead into community recreational work and feel that he is important to American defense.

A nation has likewise to broaden the vocational education of its people. It has to make unskilled people skilled, too narrowly trained individuals more broadly trained. It has to build a nation of men and women able to do jobs and do them efficiently. Here, again, is a chance for patriotic service. Men who are proud of their skills in business or industry can be induced to lend themselves for this purpose. Women who have the power that comes of possession can lend their power to the furtherance of this service.

One of the worst evils we shall have to guard against in wartime is mass hysteria. The best way to guard against such hysteria is to train people who might readily become its sources to be its preventers and allayers. It is like training children how to march out of a burning school building. Many a boy who might easily make his dash down the stairways and thus create deadly panic can be trained to self-control by being taught how to marshal the smaller children and guide them down to safety.

All adults need to be trained to know the sources, symptoms, and dangers of mass hysteria, and need to be given an understanding of the various ways in which such hysteria can be prevented or can be allayed when once it begins to manifest itself. Such training would involve a learning of the ways in which suspicion can be aroused about innocent people in a community; the ways in which rumors of spies or *saboteurs* can be started and sweep through a community; the ways in which irresponsible words can strike a spark of hatred that will grow into a conflagration. Such training should be for all citizens. Not all will need it, but if some who might easily become hysterical and so rouse hysteria in others can be induced to know about its innocent beginnings and tragic endings, less of this ugly social neurosis may be expected to develop.

This will be particularly true if we can find ways in which otherwise inconspicuous individuals may be given positions of responsibility in preventing rumors from spreading and hatreds from being generated. We might call them "Panic Police," or "Morale Wardens." It would not greatly matter what we called them so long as they could feel that their job had vital importance for preserving steadiness and self-control among their fellow Americans.

Every war draws a sharp line between citizens and aliens. It even draws a line between native citizen and foreign-born citizen. The dangers involved in war tend to give us all too easily a case of nerves. We look suspiciously to the right and left of us, at this unfamiliar face and at that. If the face is not only unfamiliar, but a little swarthier of skin than ours; if the haircut is obviously not of the American sort; if the trousers bag in a way that is not the fashion in conventional circles, we take a second look. Perhaps behind that foreign getup a foe is lurking! One of the worst disgraces of the last war was the unnecessary cruelty visited not only upon innocent foreigners, but upon citizens with foreign names. This must not happen again. The best way to prevent it will be to enlist a large number of our people in a service that protects such people from persecution. All citizens should receive instruction as to the rights of foreigners and the obligation of a democratic people to protect these rights. Many of these citizens should be enrolled as Alien Defense Counselors. Their duties should be to make themselves thoroughly acquainted with the foreigners in their district, win their confidence, help to resolve their bewilderments, and bring every case of persecution swiftly to the attention of a central board of Defense Counselors. If democracy is to prove itself better than the bestial systems of the dictators, it must even lean over backwards to be generous to all its people, even to the strangers in its midst.

Total war calls for total service. If we are wise, we shall, in a time of crisis, encourage a wide participation of our citizenry in this total service. People are always proud to do war work. It is too dangerous to let them have nothing to do. They will find something. We have to forestall the mischief of idle hands by making these hands busy in the doing of things that are good to do. If the doing of them brings honor and distinction, we need have less fear that there will be a turning to ways of ugliness. Nor ought we feel, in providing these ways, that we are merely sidetracking weaker personalities from evil ways into good. What we are doing is what we should have done long ago: giving legitimate outlets to people's tenacious wish to count for something as members of a human society.

# Part Three

# NEW SKILLS TO LEARN

* *II* *

# THE DISCIPLINE OF OUR AIMS

## I

IF WAR comes there need be no fear about what Americans will do. What we rather need to fear is what peace does to Americans. Peace seems to have no mobilizing power. It lets us go our separate ways, to attend, with complete absorption, to our separate affairs. We of the democracies believe in peace as the true way of life; but we seem unable to make peace into a socially devoted and socially energizing way of life.

In a sense, it is one of the profound tragedies of man's life that his devotion to a cause, his forgetfulness of self, his willingness to take risks for something beyond himself, are achieved for the most part only when war threatens. It gives ground for a dangerous belief that only through war is man ennobled. If this is true, then the best of all social programs will be one which calls for bigger and better wars. This is the program suggested by the fascist dictators. The way of democratic peace, they scornfully tell us, is the way to individual selfishness, individual irresponsibility, and social degeneration.

There is only one reply that we of the democracies can give: we have to prove that peace can be as profoundly arousing as war. If, among us as a people, it is not as arousing, we have to find out how it can be made so. Obviously we do not want peace to stir people in the same manner in which war stirs them. War arouses people through fears, hates, and lies. Peace must arouse them through something else.

The deep problem of democracy is to find this something else. As yet it has found it only among a few devoted people. The task of democracy is to spread the valiant spirit of these few throughout all its people. At present the millions among us are still cheerfully absorbed in their own affairs, are unaware of the obligation they owe to the bettering of the world, are complacently acquiescent in an order of things not good enough even for themselves.

How can we of the democracies match the dictators in the mobilizing of our minds, the sharpening of our aims, the toughening of our wills?

The answer would seem to lie in making the citizens of a democracy come alive to the peacetime war that is being waged in their midst. It is a many-sided war, a war fought on many battlefields. Chiefly it is an unpublicized war. Its battles are recorded as ordinary news of the day. Its soldiers wear no uniforms and carry no weapons, save the weapons of mind and spirit. But it is a war that requires courage, devotion, and alert strategy. This peacetime war is no child's business. It is business for strong men and women.

For example, there is the determined fight—waged on many fronts—to clean up political corruption. This certainly is no war for weaklings. Wherever such work is undertaken, days and nights must be spent in the difficult task of persuading people out of their easy content, out of their lazy unwillingness to bestir themselves into effort; of arousing them to resist scoundrels and put them out of control. Individuals who are out to defeat political gangsters take their life in their own hands. They have to possess at least as high an order of courage as is required on the battlefield. But they have also to possess something higher—a will not merely to destroy but to build. Deeper and more persistent than their hatred of political gangsters must be their love of decency and ordered freedom.

This is one kind of war that a peacetime democracy carries on. They who are engaged in this war, in dozens and scores of places throughout the land, are its peacetime soldiers.

Democracy carries on its peacetime war in many

other ways. For a long time now workers have been fighting for their right to have an equal voice in the government of their lives. Their fight has been their own, but it has also been democracy's fight. It has been the strong effort to turn democracy into something more than an empty platitude by making it operate in the day-by-day interests and activities of working people. The labor fight, too, has not been one for weaklings. Sometimes it has taken on a violence not pleasant to contemplate. But the long history of the labor struggle is the history of courageous men and women devoting themselves, body and soul, to a cause worth fighting for.

Another phase of democracy's peacetime war has been the struggle with disease. There is no more glorious page in the history of heroism than that which contains the story of Major Walter Reed and his humble followers of the ranks in their efforts to eradicate yellow fever. Paul de Kruif's books—*Microbe Hunters, Men Against Death, Why Keep Them Alive?, The Fight for Life*—are chronicles of high-minded devotion. It is worth remembering that democracy provides example after example of this willingness of men to sacrifice themselves in the search for that which may save their fellows. Such willingness is not commanded; it is the full response of free men to the needs of their fellow men. It is a heroism more thrilling than that of the dive-bomber. The latter harks back to the savage in us; the former moves forward to what is potential within us.

Another peacetime fight has been in behalf of the underprivileged. Jane Addams carried the shining weapons of her spirit into the dark places of Halsted Street, Chicago. She fought a fight as hard as any soldier ever fights—with crooked politicians, mean-minded slum owners, with gangsters and pimps, and with unscrupulous representatives of vested interests. It was a year-by-year fight from which she never rested. But she won her victory—as much of a victory as could be won in a land in which the exploitation of the common people was the expected way of economic and political life. Many heroic souls followed behind her banner, took her fight to other cities and other slums. Today this army continues to do its fighting—men and women who care enough about defenseless people to stand up in their defense.

Lawyers have taken up arms in the peacetime war of democracy. Many a lawyer has seen the plight of poor people and has freely given his services in their behalf. The establishment of the Legal Aid Society, with its branches throughout the land, is indication of the kind of devotion that men and women of the law have been willing to give to their less fortunate fellows. Equality before the law has been one of the vaunted principles of our democracy. But in large measure it is more honored in the breach than in the observance. The poor man gets short shrift in comparison with the man of wealth. Were it not for the devoted services of these lawyers, democracy would have but a sorry tale to tell of equal justice to all.

There is also democracy's peacetime war against ignorance. Early in our history there were those who fought for the right of common people to have an education. It was a hard and bitter fight, with the power of wealth and social status arrayed against the fighters. Today our wide-flung system of public education is tangible evidence that the battle was won. Now the warfare goes on in a new way. It is the ignorance of adults that we now fear. A new world has crowded in upon us; and our school-bred minds are far from being adequate to the task of assessing its values. Adults need to learn—to learn with their adult minds. In this case those who do the fighting face the deadliest of all enemies—apathy. It is deadly because intangible. It is negative, a cipher. Adults just do not want to learn—they have had enough of learning already. They think they know all they need to know.

All over the land—in village, town, and city—men and women devote their time and strength in the ardent effort to persuade grown-up people that old dogs need to learn new tricks. It is a stiff fight, full of setbacks, always on the brink of total defeat. But these men and women struggle along just the same, determined that the zest to keep mentally alive and growing shall some day be the accepted way of adult life.

## II

This—in all its many-sidedness—is democracy's peacetime war. To the average mind it seems nothing to get excited about. It has no slogans, no hate-rousing songs, no marchings, no embarkations and farewells. It has no "definiteness."

The clue, perhaps, is in this word. Democracy's peacetime war has no definiteness. It is everywhere and it is of all kinds—in schools, colleges, forums, civic associations, nonpartisan leagues, laboratories, labor unions, consumers' co-operatives, slum-clearance projects, crime commissions. It has nothing of the satisfying clarity of a single enemy, a single heroic job to be done.

Totalitarianism mobilizes the aims and wills of its people for one definite thing; it shapes them to one common denominator of feeling and purpose. If the common denominator turns out to be a *least* common denominator—fear and hatred—the arousal is nonetheless powerful.

This is the "total" way: one pattern, one desire, one will. All together! If it is to be toward monstrous killing, then it is the same killing for all. If it is toward a monstrous lie, then it is the same lie for all. Democracy is different. Descriptive of its way of life is the phrase *e pluribus unum*. Democracy seeks unity, but it does not seek it by reducing all to one denominator of feeling and intention. It seeks unity out of the co-operation of many freedoms and many devotions.

The mobilizing of aims in a democracy must, then, be a very different thing from the mobilizing of them in a totalitarian country. Democracy must allow for many different ways in which many different individuals may serve a common good. It must not expect the kind of arousal that is accompanied by the "hip, hip, hoorah" of a mass response. Its arousals must be in the inwardness of single persons who see what needs to be done and go and do it.

## III

To the ardent mind that sees the evil of modern society to be one and one only—the evil of maldistribution of wealth—all this is uninspiring. Such a mind wants to get to the root of all our evils and to strike at that root. Such a mind wants a "total" war—a war of all against one identical deadly thing.

It would indeed be inspiring if we could wage such

a war; if we could find the single root of our evils and strike it dead. But to many of us puzzled ones there seems to be no such single root. Life is more like a banyan tree that grows from many roots and sends down its branches to form more roots. We have to hack away at hundreds of roots and still the evil is not disposed of.

It is a hard lesson that the democratic mind has to learn: that there is no one great obvious thing to achieve to make democracy work. There are thousands of things that have to be achieved. The adolescent mind characteristically thinks in terms of spectacular adventure. Every lore of primitive folk has its tale of the hero who goes forth to kill the dragon. It is always *the* dragon—not a lot of them. And when the hero returns, everybody lives happily ever after. It would be easy if life were like that. Life, however, is much more complex, and much less spectacular. It is a day-by-day "doing of a lot of little things in a lot of little places by a lot of little people."

Perhaps our weakness as a democratic people is that we are still in the adolescent stage. We wait for the call of the *one really great adventure*. If and when that call comes we shall, of course, be there. Meanwhile, since the call to mobilize has not yet come, we go about our own business.

To become a fighter in the democratic cause, one has to be willing to stay at home and do the next thing that needs to be done. For no place where people live and work together—home, school, village, town, city, nation—yet measures up to the dreams that possess us. As long as there are unfulfillments in any situation, the call of a democracy to its citizens is to mobilize their creative thinking in the effort to turn unfulfillment into fulfillment.

One very real weakness of our democracy is that we have not dramatized the peacetime war that we are having to wage along all fronts. We have read military history, and our minds have been conditioned to the heroism that goes forth in uniforms to win military glory. We have done nothing—or next to nothing—to dramatize for ourselves the profounder heroism of unpublicized men and women who fight the daily, many-sided fight against unspectacular evil, and who fight their fight not for the glory of military citations but for the satisfaction of a more decent life for all.

We need to learn how to do this dramatizing; how to build up a pride in the thousandfold betterings of life; how to induce more people in more ways, with their free minds, to get at the human jobs that need to be undertaken. We need to learn how to be inspired to devote our energies to at least one hard job of human betterment.

A nation made up of individuals, each one engaged in at least one good hard fight for a thing worth while, would be a nation collectively engaged in the only kind of war worth fighting.

# * 12 *

## PUTTING TENACITY INTO OUR HOPES

TODAY we are again making the familiar resolution: "We must build a better world." But how does one build a better world? What are the specific things we have to do in order to go about the building of it? Most people, when they think of a possibly more civilized future, merely have a sad ache inside them and a vague wish to have things different.

If we of this tragic generation are to do anything to end the succession of man's follies, we shall have to put some iron of discipline into our hopes. We shall have to stop being vaguely wishful, to cease making noble verbal gestures about a warless future. We shall have to do the hard, prosaic work of thinking out, in detail, what we expect a more decent order of life to be.

It is like a prospective home builder who asks himself the question: "What kind of a house do I want to build?" He does not go about with a pious wish to have a nice house. He may, to be sure, leave it all to an architect; or he may buy a house ready-made. But such a home builder is a weak brother. He is not passionately interested in a house. He chiefly wants a roof over his head and an escape from the bother of thinking about it. If someone else can do the thinking for him, so much the better.

The real home builder has a passion that possesses him. One can find him in every spare moment of his time (more likely it is a "her"), digging into home-building magazines for floor plans, exterior finishes, designs of interior decoration. One can find him visiting architectural exhibits, ferreting out building materials, heating plants, kitchen equipment, lighting fixtures. In all likelihood he keeps a notebook of house ideas, or a special drawer into which he crowds clippings from newspapers and articles from magazines. The passion-possessed home builder, in short, spends his time getting his future house *in detail* long before he ventures to call in an architect to do the expert designing.

We who care about a more decent society have to do something like that. Plans for a better society are no small thing to be tossed off in a conversation over a cup of coffee, or in a lecture from a platform. We have to dig into all the facts we can learn about human beings, about how they behave and what they need, and about the forms of association that are most likely to succeed.

First and foremost, however, we have to be keenly aware of the mistakes we have made. At an architectural exhibit in California, called "Telesis," a group of exhibiting architects made a display of the inexcusable uglinesses found in our modern cities and countrysides. They placed over these the caption: IS THIS THE BEST WE CAN DO? These architects were doing the first thing that needs to be done in contemplation of a future society: they were looking at present civilization *in detail*, and asking, in every case, "Is this the best we can do?"

It suggests a first step in self-discipline for all of us. Substitute for the usual vague and sweeping condemnation of our civilization ("it's ugly"; or "it's unjust"; or "it's materialistic") a point-by-point examination of behaviors and environments and a point-by-point discovery of the things we believe ought not to be carried into the society we are hoping to help build. This is a salutary and difficult exercise. It makes one look more closely at the things one has taken for granted; for example, this Negro boy condemned for life to menial service (shall we import this race snobbishness into our new society?); this high-school student at military drill, learning the art of shooting his fellow men (shall we build war expectations among the young in our new society?); this college professor teaching economics out of books (do we want students to get life out of books or to make their own books out of contact with life?); this minister of the gospel serving comforting platitudes to the comfortable (do we want soporific and self-congratulatory churches?); these houses that are airless, sunless, gardenless (do we want our urban monstrosities continued?); these women at endless bridge parties (do we want an upper middle class of leisurely futilitarians?); this cheap radio stuff (do we want to keep our people on the level of infants?).

This is an enlivening question to carry around with one: "Is this the best we can do?" A daily dozen of exercises with this question will make one come alive with a detailed understanding of what we do not and ought not to want in a future society. We need, in short, to draw up a bill of particulars so that we shall become clear in our own minds as to the specific things we *do not* want in our future world.

It is needless to say that almost no one does this. Our schools ought to teach young people how to do it—not, indeed, to make cranks or cynics out of them, but to enliven and give point to their observations. It is a pity that schools have, in general, to gear their teaching to the psychology of the community booster. It is an equal pity that they have to think of patriotism only as an attitude of approval. The sincerest patriotism may require drastic things to be said about one's country or one's community or one's people. Better to have young people say drastic things because, with their own eyes, they have seen things to be drastic about, than to have them repeat melancholy cynicisms that adolescents love but that come out of no experience of their own.

This is the first thing we need to do if we are to think capably about a better society. There is then this second thing: we need to accumulate, day by day, specific ideas about arrangements in a more decent society. The first requisite for this second stage is resolutely to refuse to use any word ending in *ism.* To say that we need socialism, or collectivism, or a modified capitalism, is as good as to say nothing. The best discipline of the mind is to break every ism down into the specific arrangements it calls for. If one has a hankering after socialism, how, specifically, does one visualize a carpenter earning his living, a farmer, a doctor, or a teacher? If one wants a modified capitalism, how does one specifically visualize the management of currency? Are its values to be subject to the arbitrary say-so of a president or of Congress? In what specific ways are the crazy fluctuations of currency to be overcome? How, if at all, are prices to be regulated? How is the marginal worker, the sharecropper, the migratory worker, the seasonal worker to be helped to an all-year-round living wage? If we could do this detailed kind of thinking; if we could, with one concerted breath, blow all the isms out of our talk and our thinking, we should be well on the way to the achievement of social intelligence.

The following may sound silly; but since nothing can be sillier than our present absence of intelligent thinking about the future, we venture the suggestion that every individual ought to keep what might be called A NOTEBOOK OF TOMORROW. In an age that moves rapidly and disconcertingly toward new things, the individual ought to keep alert to the directions in which he wants his world to move. His notebook should be the record of the day-by-day turning of his mind toward the future. It should be a growing accumulation of his specific ideas of what he thinks the world of tomorrow should be. If at the end of six months he has nothing but blank pages, he can turn his critical eyes upon himself and tell himself that, as far as future-mindedness is concerned, he is a total loss. Many of us are total losses; but, unfortunately, we have no blank pages to apprise us of the humiliating fact. So we go on with our vaporous platitudinizing as if we knew what we were talking about.

I know of no substitute for the two kinds of thinking outlined above—thinking about specific defects and about specific new arrangements. They are the only exercises I know that will keep our minds alert and disciplined about the human future.

But more than this, they are exercises that will keep

our wills from slackening. As we have said, in tragic days we resolve to build a better world; but when the tragic days are over, our wills begin to slacken and our resolutions peter out. There is no help in our merely saying to ourselves, "We must keep our resolves." Other matters capture our attention and inevitably we slide into forgetfulness. It seems that there is only one way to keep a resolve alive; namely, continually to do things that advance the resolve. Thus, we advance our resolve to build a better world by doing detailed day-by-day thinking about how that better world may be organized and *putting our thinking into black and white.* The putting into black and white requires an exercise of will and a sharpening of attention. After a while such day-by-day thinking and such day-by-day writing down of our thoughts build up a habit. There arrives a time, then, when the thinking itself becomes second nature, a time when we simply cannot *not* think about this thing that possesses us.

In other words, resolves peter out when our attention peters out. If we keep the attention, we keep the resolve. There is no reason why it should be true that our moments of high resolution should always end in futile forgetfulness. If we are wisely persistent in the focusing and the holding of our attention, our high resolves can be built into the permanent fabric of our life.

# * 13 *

# BUILDING A NEW TRADITION OF LEARNING

## I

IN ONE sense, Americans are a highly intelligent people. Doctors, lawyers, merchants, secretaries, carpenters, chemists—each one of these is intelligent in his special area of expertness. But a democratic nation has to be more than a nation of intelligent specialists.

Democracy implies that people are—or ought to be—the rulers of their common destiny. In a democracy, therefore, each individual has to perform two functions: to earn a living by his specialized expertness, and to join with his fellow specialists in shaping the policies for their common life. We might call the first of these functions vocational, the second societal. Obviously, the typical failures of Americans are in the areas of societal thinking.

If we ask why the failures, the answer would seem to be a simple one. For a long time we have carried on the education of our people with a singular psychological obtuseness. We still do this. We educate them to societal understanding—through history, literature, economics—in those years when they are still too immature to grasp the full significance of what they study. Then, when their minds reach maturity, and when, if given the chance, they *could* grasp the significance of these societal matters, we encourage in them an exclusive absorption in their vocations. Thus, while we succeed in making them vocationally mature, we keep them societally immature.

Psychologically, the case against this procedure is so clear it would seem to need only to be stated to be acted on. But we follow here an old tradition that we cannot seem to break; namely, that everything which needs to be known about our world of human relationships can be learned in the years when we are young. In those years we implant the knowledge of right and wrong, of the processes of government, of the structure and practices of business and industry, of the historical steps by which our present civilization has emerged out of past orders of life. In the Sunday school we implant a knowledge of God and of man's relation to Him.

All of this teaching, we assume, can be successfully done in the immature years. Our belief embodies itself in the thousands of elementary and high-school buildings throughout the land where such societal teaching is carried on. That the tradition is completely accepted by us is indicated by the fact that nowhere throughout America—save in a few places—can we find a building devoted to the teaching of societal wisdom to adults. Education for societal thinking, we still believe, is for juveniles; education for vocational thinking is for adults.

What is most surprising about this educational tradition is that it assumes societal thinking to be easy thinking, and hence appropriate for juveniles. Actually it is the hardest thinking of all—far harder than vocational thinking, for it involves an understanding of the profound complexities and uncertainties of human nature.

This is one reason why history, economics, politics, religion, and the rest, taught to juvenile minds, have been so disappointing in their results. These subjects have had to be oversimplified and sugar-coated. The simple code of right and wrong taught to youngsters is far from being thorough enough to resolve the intricate problems of adulthood. The simple story of governments—monarchies, oligarchies, republics—is too superficial to give youngsters a sense of the perplexing interplay of psychological and economic forces to make their juvenile knowledge useful in adulthood. The simple economics of supply and demand, land, rent, and capital that a high-school student learns is far from giving him a sense of the maddening complexity of the processes that actually occur in the world of business, industry, and finance. At best, he gets some fairly platitudinous notions about initiative, enterprise, integrity, and ambition—which he will later repeat with ignorant unction. The simple history he learns—of dynasties and battles—is far from giving him a sense of the deep and perplexing social forces that slowly shape the destinies of peoples. He learns to think in Hollywood fashion—in terms of gunplay and glamour; and he is pretty much unprepared to know what it is, in human history, that makes for man's defeats and triumphs. The literature he reads, profoundly searching as it may be in its analysis of human motives and behaviors, enters a mind still unprepared to appreciate its subtleties. Finally, the simple religion he learns in Sunday school is too much like a fairy tale—of a beneficent God that gives gifts to His obedient children—to serve the hard needs of a difficult world, where religion must take the maturer form of visiting the fatherless and the widows in their affliction. In adulthood, this means not the complacent Sunday-religion found in far too many churches, but the weekday religion of straightening out injustices and allaying the sorrows of the world.

Let any person of mature years try to recall what he got out of his high-school study of the history of Greece; or out of his high-school study of Shakespeare;

or even out of his college study of economics. If this person of mature years has happened recently to take up the study of Greece, or of Shakespeare, or of economics, he will recall the amazed new insights of his mature mind. "Why," he will say, "we only studied a few facts about Grecian history and never knew even what they were about. Why the Greeks had problems! They were a living people, fumbling with perplexities, fooled by charlatans, greedy and noble, wise and foolish." He will recall similar amazed insights if, in his recent years, he has taken up the study of Shakespeare or of economics.

There are millions of adults who know societal matters only as they have studied them in high school or college. Can we expect their knowledge to be deep and detailed enough for adult life? Obviously, what they know—of history, or political science, or economics—in their forties and fifties will be only the ragtags of their immature learning. Unfortunately, they will not know these to be ragtags. Never having learned otherwise, they will think they are the real thing.

If we could make a composite picture of the inside of the minds of mature people who have been "educated" in the schools and colleges, we should find a picture of disconnected dates and happenings, half-known personages, and misconceived relationships. No more than one can make a silk purse out of a sow's ear can one create mature understanding of human relationships out of immature minds.

## II

Here lies perhaps the gravest problem of our democracy. These people around us—bankers, merchants, artists, mechanics—who look so mature, but who are, in their societal education, so immature, are the free minds that are supposed to rule in a free society. Obviously, such minds are not fit for the job. To be sure, they have managed, in a way, to do the job; but this has simply been because of the good fortune of our circumstances. Nature has hitherto been generous enough in her resources to take care of our societal blunders.

We live today in a close-packed, close-related society, where blunders have world-wide repercussions. A free society today has to have minds maturely disciplined to know the things they need to know about people, their activities and their relations, in a worldwide society.

This means that we shall have to depart from old traditions. We shall have to change the little red schoolhouse into the big community schoolhouse. There adults as well as juveniles will have to go to learn the things that each, at his age level, needs to learn.

At the present time we are taking a few steps in this

direction. We have forums and study circles in many of our cities and towns, and adult centers in a few of them. And a Town Meeting of the Air is rousing millions of adults to think about our common problems. The strength of such groups is that they create situations in which people are trained to consider all sorts of questions, to be fair in their expressions of ideas, and to demand fairness of others. In such groups we can detect tomorrow's adult education in the making. Their weakness is that they are still too incidental—too much apart from our daily life—to serve as a unified educational discipline for our people. Also, quite innocently, they often help to perpetuate the illusion that societal thinking is easy, that all we need to do is to talk out our social problems for an hour or so and go home with safe conclusions.

We shall have to call such activities good without calling them good enough. Listening to a lecture on European entanglements, or sitting in on a discussion of money and credit, can at best be only a beginning. If we want to know about these things—and we have to—we must dig into the problems, precisely as any student of engineering has to dig into his mathematics and his physics before he can expect to function as an engineer.

This is hard doctrine. Adults do not like it. Having once been graduated, they thank God that all that is over. They do not want to go back to school or forward to any new kind of school. They want to be on their own. This is America speaking, adult America, with the right, by gosh, to go about its own affairs!

But if America keeps on speaking that way too long, America, with all its specialized intelligence, will find itself to be a nation of people too ignorant to be wise governors of themselves. These are days that not only try men's souls but challenge their minds. What we suffer from chiefly is not sheer, unadulterated evil that has come from somewhere across the water. We suffer, rather, from sheer ignorance as to how to manage our own affairs. What we need, therefore, is citizen-intelligence—hard-bitten, disciplined, grown-up citizen-intelligence. We shall not have such intelligence if adults, millions of them, continue to remain, in societal matters, millions of juveniles.

Our best defense, then, against ceasing to be what we wish to be as a democracy, is to begin, as a people, building a tradition of education as a process that gets more and more significant the older we become. It gets more and more significant because each year adds to our experience. Each gives new background for what we learn. Each gives us added power to check facts and opinions against what we ourselves have learned of life. Each gives us an added chance to make judgments that are mature.

A COMMUNITY-WIDE SCHOOL FOR EVERY COMMUNITY: This would be a good slogan for an America that faces the new alternative of having either to make all its people intelligent or to seek directive intelligence from a dictator.

In a modern democracy great issues cannot be settled by the cracker-barrel technique. The great issues of today need sustained and disciplined thinking. We American adults, therefore, will have to go to school. This will require humility on our part. For to go to school means, in a sense, a surrender. It means a surrender to man's long efforts of honest exploration. It means giving up the right to prejudices and easy dogmatisms. It means giving up cocksureness. It means, in short, in the deepest sense of that phrase, becoming "as a little child." The curious paradox is that when an adult becomes as a little child—ready to learn—he then becomes genuinely adult. America now needs mental and emotional adults.

# 14

# TAKING CHARGE OF OUR WORDS

## I

"LET the words of our mouths . . . be acceptable." This is the prayer that genuine maturity makes. For the mature person, who has witnessed the misunderstandings and conflicts of people, knows that words can be deadly weapons in the hands both of the careless and of the unscrupulous. If the beginning of wisdom is fear of the Lord, the next step in wisdom should be fear of the misuse of the word.

The misuse of words by the unscrupulous is bad enough; but their misuse by the innocent is worse. It is the innocent misuse of words that we wish here to consider.

Words are most mischievous when they are accepted by us as substitutes for things. Let me give an example. I have at hand a report of a comparison of beliefs of high-school students and enrollees of C.C.C. camps.

"Almost half of our young people of both school and camp," the report reads, "believe that we should blame the invention of machinery for unemployment." This belief looks like an *idea* on the part of these young people. It looks like something they have reasoned out. But an idea, to be reasoned out correctly, should stem from direct experience. How widely have these young people traced the connection between unemployment and the invention of machinery? The obvious answer is that they have not traced it at all. They may have seen a few displacements of individuals by machines; but in all likelihood they have merely heard certain words that have gone the rounds. They have heard people say, "Machinery is the cause of unemployment," and have accepted these words as the expression of reality. As a result they have a glib explanation for unemployment. "They are willing," the report continues, "to blame anything for unemployment except social shortsightedness." In short, the easy words they have accepted turn their minds away from the only explanation that would seem really to explain. Thereafter, in complete innocence, they will blame machinery, when, as a matter of fact, they ought to be worrying their heads off about "social shortsightedness." Lulled by words, they will go into their adult life, prepared to make no effort to discover how and why our minds go wrong. They will—like millions of our fellow citizens–accept an easy explanation that is no explanation at all.

This illustrates one mischief that words can do. They can turn us aside from real explanations. They can send us chasing after false clues. They can make us think we are hot on the trail of truth when we are only heading into a blind alley. The report continues: "They . . . have a mystic reverence for 'energy' and 'ambition.' . . . The great majority believe that 'there is always room at the top.' . . . In spite of the fact that they themselves and most of their parents are out of work, they still believe that 'any energetic and ambitious person can get a job.' "

One can already predict the latter end of these young people: they will pertinaciously believe that everything is really sound in our economic and social order, and that the trouble is only with lazy and ambitionless individuals. They will vote for the party that stands for the old virtues of rugged self-reliance and will stubbornly refuse to consider ways of readjusting our economic and social arrangements to the new needs of human beings.

Again they have taken words for things. For these young people have made no wide and searching effort to find out whether there *is* always room at the top, whether energy and ambition always *do* win out. They have merely heard certain words. They have believed these words as if they were the reality itself.

This is why people cannot seem to think straight about social issues. They have so grown the habit of letting words be substitutes for things that they have lost the habit of looking straight and hard at things themselves.

The discipline of our minds in respect to words must involve, first, a solemn promise to ourselves that we will not make high-sounding pronouncements unless we have made enough observations to back up our words, or unless we are reporting observations that we can fully trust. This would dispose of at least 90 per cent of our political speeches, and perhaps 75 per cent of all heated arguments on social and economic issues. It would close our mouths and stop our pens until we had something to say that came straight from our experience, or from the experience of those in whose scientific integrity we had reason to have confidence.

When an unscrupulous person uses words, he intends to do damage to someone else. When an innocent person misuses words in the ways above described, he innocently does damage to himself. Francis Bacon expressed it thus: "Words, as a Tartar bow, do shoot back upon the understanding of the wisest, and mightily entangle and pervert the judgment." It is this innocent self-perversion of our judgment by the words we so easily pick up in books, newspapers, and conversation that makes sound social thinking have such hard sledding.

## II

Words can, if we let them, send us chasing after false clues. They can also do another thing that is mischievous. They can seem to address themselves to our minds when in reality they shoot past our minds and hit quite another part of our anatomy. Words can have emotional overtones. "American" rings a bell in us. If we call a plan an "American plan" we are all set to accept it even without examination. Unscrupulous people use the word and fool us. But, also, we tend to fool ourselves. If we can say to ourselves that this is an "American way" of doing things, we have a warm feeling aroused in us. The word shoots past our minds and lodges in our affections.

There are many words of this kind, words, as Kipling once said, that "may become alive and walk up and down in the hearts of the hearers." It is good to have words walk up and down in our hearts; but first they should walk up and down in our heads. "Democracy" is one such word. We like it and accept it —and think only shallowly of what it means. If we can say to ourselves that we are a democracy and that those other nations are dictatorships, this is enough for us. The issue is settled.

Once we start thinking of what democracy means in our actual experience, it may not, however, look so bright to us. We may then see it as a thing of rags and tatters, of hypocrisies and evasions. We may then see it as only half-formed, as striving to be something it is not yet. When we thus pass the word from our hearts to our heads, something sobering happens. The first fine, careless rapture goes, but hard-bitten determination follows.

Hitler is a master artist at shooting past people's heads and hitting their hearts. The words he uses are emotion-words: "blood and race," "home," "work," "strength through joy," "heroism," "the good old German way." He has all his people cheering. This is what they want—the good, warm feeling inside. The heads take a holiday.

Anger-words are equally mischievous. They hit the adrenals. They start the heart pumping and the blood racing. They, too, shoot past the head. Politicians love to use them: "agitators," "aliens," "stirrers-up of class hatred," "unpatriotic slackers." The fact that they can be shouted and will get instant response is indication enough that they shoot straight to the adrenals. If they were addressed to the minds of people, they would induce the delayed response which is the sign that thinking is going on.

We need, therefore, to discipline ourselves in the use of emotion-arousing words, or "emotive" words, as they are called by the students of semantics. We need to take a solemn vow not to direct such words either to the hearts or the adrenals of other people unless at the same time we direct them to their heads. And we need to take a similar vow in defense of ourselves. We need to pass such words through the corridors of our minds before we let them pass into the deeper places of our affections and our angers.

## III

Not long ago I had a revealing experience in one of my college classes. The boys had been discussing a chapter in H. G. Wells's *Anatomy of Frustration.* Let me say, by way of preface, that I had been sufficiently impressed by the book to assign it as a major text in a class in social philosophy. Although I thought highly of the book, because it attempted what to me seemed a penetrating exploration of our human weaknesses, the students were increasingly at outs with it. In fact, they treated the book with downright disgust—a disgust in which I, as assigner of the volume, was generously included. I guessed that the reason for the disgust was that Mr. Wells offered no clear-cut program for social reconstruction. He was bent, rather, upon revealing the confusions in our minds, the antisocial effects of our egoisms and egotisms, rationalizations, and self-deceptions. One day the disgust seemed to reach a climax. For about an hour all kinds of discussional brickbats were thrown at him, and almost every one of the brickbats carried with it the word "liberal." There were a few students who used the word in a eulogistic sense; most of them employed it as a term of opprobrium.

Not being the Walrus, I felt that the time had come to cease talking about many things and to talk about one thing only. I asked the class to define what they meant by "a liberal." We still had another hour to go. In that hour the disclosure of our own confusions and misunderstandings was so vivid that the class and I emerged a chastened and illuminated group.

The definitions came like shots from a Gatling gun. I set them down here, not as examples of good definitions, nor even of what students believe to be good definitions, but as expressions of the emotional diversity that can be contained in a word that is bandied about with the most careless unconcern.

1. A liberal is one who continually sits on the fence.
2. A liberal is one who is opposed to authority.
3. A liberal is one who believes in free speech.

4. A liberal is one who has a mental attitude opposed to dogmas of all kinds.
5. A liberal is one who believes in scientific method.
6. A liberal is one who is completely tolerant.
7. A liberal is one who is humanitarian; that is, interested in social problems.
8. A liberal is one who does not believe he has the final answer.
9. A liberal is one who is completely open-minded.
10. A liberal is one who thinks about social questions, but does not act.

Obviously what was troubling many of these students (note 1, 6, 9, 10) was the conception of the liberal as a person who never can make up his mind, who is too timid to decide and to act, who is a shilly-shallyer in times of crisis; in short, one who is so open-minded that he is a sieve. On the other hand, among other students there was enough appreciation of the social-mindedness of the liberal, his unwillingness to be dogmatic, his wish to listen before deciding, to make them defend him as a desirable type.

When these hit-and-miss definitions were all on the blackboard, we decided that in spite of the differences there might be some underlying common quality on which we could agree, so that henceforth when we used the word we should use it with this quality in mind. We saw, of course, that the whole previous hour of acrimonious discussion had really been an hour of unconsciously and futilely arguing at cross-purposes.

We therefore set to work to find what we were thereafter to mean when we used the word "liberal." It took the rest of that hour to bring forth our little mouse of definition from our mountain of confusion. When it finally appeared it was shaped as follows: "A liberal is one who seeks to apply scientific method to the solution of social problems." This definition ruled out all the bitterness about sitting forever on the fence, being innocently open to all ideas, thinking and never acting. We decided that although these attitudes might be present in certain individuals, the essential thing about a liberal is his persistent use of intelligence—rather than force or emotion or subterfuge—to advance human affairs.

Not a very exciting definition—but it was at least one upon which we could agree. Thereafter we knew—or ought to have known—what we meant to be talking about when we used the word. We had turned an emotion-laden word of diverse meanings into some semblance of logical preciseness. And thereby we had made intelligent discussion possible.

## IV

The difficulty during that first hour in my classroom was that there was no chance for a genuine meeting of minds. It was as if a chemist were to talk about the properties of calcium, when a fellow chemist to whom he was talking thought he was speaking of potassium. This seldom happens in the region of laboratories. There a word means what, by expert agreement, it is meant to mean. In our ordinary converse, however, words mean what each of us wants them to mean and wants the other fellow to want them to mean. We remember Humpty Dumpty in *Through the Looking-Glass:*

"When I use a word," Humpty Dumpty said in a rather scornful tone, "it means just what I choose it to mean—neither more nor less."

"The question is," said Alice, "whether you can make words mean so many different things."

"The question is," said Humpty Dumpty, "which is to be master—that's all."

What was revealed in my class, however, was not merely a diversity of meaning in a single word. There was revealed, also, the end result of that curious process whereby a word becomes a stereotype. Before that particular discussion, the word "liberal," to many of my students, evoked an image. It was the image of a timid, indecisive, Hamlet-like individual. That image was so vivid that it halted thinking. The image occupied the forefront of consciousness and made it quite unnecessary to check the word against the facts. Are all liberals like that? Has the word ever been used in another sense? Are there people now who actually use the word differently? The vivid image of the indecisive Hamlet crowded out all such thoughts, and the mind responded instantly to one very narrow, emotion-laden meaning. It is significant to note that in some communities the word "liberal" connotes a wild-eyed radical.

This process of turning good, honest concepts into stereotypes goes on among us all the time. It is perhaps the chief source of our inability to come to intelligent understanding of one another, or even to an intelligent discussion of common problems. It is frequently maintained that we are unable to make much advance toward a more civilized life because we are selfish—or even downright cruel. My own observations seem not to confirm this view. Most people, as I know them, are fairly decent. They are not consciously and deliberately "exploiters" (another stereotype), or "grinders of the faces of the poor," or sadistic "warmongers."

One reason we advance so slowly, it seems to me—it is, of course, far from being the only one—is that even the best and most generous of us fail to understand one another. Let one of my colleagues mention "collectivism" to some of my farm friends in the West, and they will think he has devil's horns concealed under his forelock. Now I have no doubt that if my colleague could be given time to tell very clearly what *he* means by collectivism, he could convince them that he does not mean what *they* mean. For them the word is a stereotype. It brings up the image of Soviet regimentation and of a cruel, bureaucratic Stalin ordering the death of the kulaks. For him, the word is a social concept. If he were to tell precisely what his meaning is, I do not doubt that they would approve of his sanity and wisdom. But as it stands now, good people in the West (and elsewhere) will not listen to this kind of talk, although this kind of talk may be just the kind we all ought to be talking.

I have been present both as speaker and as listener in scores of forum meetings. I have heard many "problems" presented and supposedly discussed. But I fail to remember any meeting (my own included) when time was taken to come to some common agreement upon the major words used. I confess that I am now doing my best as, in this matter, I begin to see the light. I think back to the dozens and dozens of times in which I have used words of crucial import that have not gone forth into my audiences as clear-cut terms, with single, precise meanings—like "cat" and "dog," "tree" and "ax"—but that have left my own lips with one meaning and have hatched in the minds of my audiences meanings so diverse as to be unrecognizable by their progenitor. No wonder the old gentleman in the corner would rise and suggest that I had missed the most important point of the discussion. As a matter of fact, he had missed what I meant. There was no use chiding the old gentleman. I knew that he had sound ideas, and that I, too, had sound ideas. What we needed was not mutual castigation, but time out to go patiently into the matter of a word that I had tried to use as a concept but that had clicked in his mind as a stereotype (or vice versa?).

Think of how we mess things up with our stereotypes. The speaker tells of "the high standard of living in America." At once an image: good, hard-working, middle-class Americans with a car in the garage and a chicken in the pot; and Japanese—or Chinese, or Austrians, or Russians, or Turks—slaving away at a miserable wage! This stereotype is achieved by persistently comparing ourselves with those less well off than we are. But suppose we compared ourselves with what we ourselves—all of us—might be. Or suppose that we chose to reveal the low standard of living of certain groups—tenant farmers, Negroes in the South, textile workers in the slums. We should then build a precise concept of what a "high standard of living" should mean. Our practice, on the contrary, is to use the term and let it go at that. If we are interested in persuading people to leave well enough alone, our stereotype is a convenient means of evoking an image that will make people whoop for the *status quo*.

"College professor" has in recent years become a convenient stereotype. I have no wish to defend my professorial fellows, but I seem to find that not all college professors are "removed from life," "theoretical, not practical," "picayunish," "academic" (which is another stereotype). They are, for the most part, interesting, well-informed men, who know a spade when they see one and are able to call it by name. But let a speaker vociferate about "college professors in politics," and the stereotype leaps into life. The stereotypic college professor may exist only in the minds of speaker and hearer, but by the stereotype shall the professor be judged!

## V

I should think that adult centers might do well to include in their curriculum one prominent course—recommended, perhaps, as indispensable—which might have a title reminiscent of the *Hunting of the Snark*. The Snark, you recall, was an unreal beast. So, too, for the most part, is the stereotypic image. Thus we might offer a course called "Hunting Stereotypes in Darkest America." This, I suppose, would never do. We might, however, call the course "How to Know Stereotypes When We Meet Them," or, more staidly, "Aids to Clear Communication." Such a course would be of great service both in protecting us against these insidious arousers of our emotion and confusers of our thought, and in training us to refrain from the unfair —or unconscious—use of them ourselves.

We might, in such a course, have researches, for example, on how "the ladder of opportunity" came to be part of our American image-making propensity, and how real and unreal the image is; a lesson on what "100 per cent American" really means when divested of its emotional connotation; lessons on how stereotypes turn into slogans and how they are used to manipulate votes —"the full dinner pail"; "high tariff for the protection of American industries"; "America for Americans" (what is America and who are the Americans who are to inherit it?); investigations into the blessed stereotype "healthy competition." "Healthy," of course, is a delightful word; it makes us feel friendly and wishful. When the orator describes our system of wasteful, hit-or-miss, profit-making scramble for the other fellow's business as healthy competition, we rest back comfortably with the feeling that God's in our economic heaven and all's right with our particular American world.

And, finally, there could be a rich, rotund lesson on name-calling stereotypes: agitator, economic royalist, Tory, militarist, pacifist, Fascist, Communist, tired radical, impractical idealist, fellow traveler. It might be said that one of the fundamental aims of all education, adult or otherwise, is to free individuals from pernicious stereotypes. At least the individual should know when he is dealing with an honest concept and when with a stereotype. Concepts are essential to our thinking. They are a form of mental shorthand. When concepts are genuine, they refer to something real. Thus, "horse" refers to real animals that can be recognized for what they are. A stereotype, on the other hand, is a concept that is not accurately descriptive. When "agitator" is applied to labor organizers, a disparaging meaning is implied that does not necessarily fit the actual persons. When "100 per cent American" is used as a term of eulogy, it pretends to describe a condition that is, in effect, not describable. There is not, and cannot be, such a creature.

We need, then, to be made vividly aware of the difference between honest concepts and dishonest stereotypes. For of the latter is the kingdom of confusion.

In lieu of special courses devoted to this end, it might well be expected of every speaker that he take some preliminary moments to state the major terms he means to use. If one of the major terms is "individualism," he should say quite frankly, "This, ladies and gentlemen, is what I am going to mean when I use the term 'individualism.' It may not be your meaning, but when I use the term, please remember how I am using it. Later in the evening there will be an opportunity to modify this meaning if modification seems called for. But while I am speaking, the word will mean thus and so, and only thus and so."

Words are the indispensable tools of our discourse. A tool must be dependable. It would be a sad state of affairs if what looked like a sturdy pair of pliers turned out in use to be a double-edged razor. But this is precisely what is constantly happening in our social use of words. The business of education is to teach us how to prevent words from slipping into multiple meanings. A word that is all things to all men is not a word; it is a social pest.

"Let the words of our mouths . . . be acceptable." I suppose this prayer is still worth praying—and it probably should be prayed on Mondays and Tuesdays as well as on Sundays. The words of our mouths can do deadly things, to ourselves as well as to others. But if the words of our mouths can be the precise expression of the meditations of our hearts, and of the accurate thinking of our heads, we shall be a little farther removed than we now are from social futility.

# Part Four
# NEW VALUES TO CREATE

★ *15* ★

# NEW DESIGNS FOR EQUALITY

## I

How can all people be made equal? It sounds like nonsense. Nature is not impartial. She distributes good brains to some and poor to others; vigorous constitutions to some and weak to others. Nature is like a gambler tossing dice—now lucky numbers, now unlucky ones. When the lucky numbers fall, they rise up and take possession of the unlucky ones. This is Nature's way; and this, inevitably, must be our human way. Equality is sentimental nonsense.

Some people never get further than this in their thinking. They see what they see: brainy persons and stupid, energetic persons and lazy; and they are unable to go beyond what their eyes see. However, they will listen approvingly to what is read to them on a Sunday: "Faith is the evidence of things not seen." They recognize the spiritual sense of this; but they do not recognize its sense in the everyday life of people.

But this is precisely the kind of faith that democracy has. It sees in people something which cannot be seen. If it says "All men are created equal," it means that, given the right conditions, all men can achieve the kind of equality that is latent within them.

Is this faith nonsense? If by equality we mean biological and psychological equality, it is. Even in a democracy, we cannot, by thought, add a cubit to our stature; nor can we change a slow, plodding brain into a swift and brilliant one. But this is not the kind of equality democracy means. When it says that all men are created equal, it means that they are created equal in the right to be what they have it in them to be.

However, this has to be said in passing on this subject of natural inequality: first, that it has been too long used as a justification for maintaining inequalities that were then used as justification for maintaining others; second, that current experiments in both nutrition and psychology are throwing such startling new light on the relationship between bodily and social well-being on the one hand, and psychological ability on the other, that our age-old excuse for letting some people be down while others are up seems on the point of leaving us altogether.

In order to realize the basic right to be what we have

it in us to be, there must be equality of opportunity. This is far from having as yet been realized. The child of a migrant worker is infinitely removed in opportunity from the child of an intelligent, socially wise, successful physician, or lawyer, or teacher. The latter child lives in an environment that allows for breadth of outlook, gives elbowroom for thought, and yields the kind of security in which generosity and considerateness can grow. What is here involved is not merely a money-difference. It is a difference, so to speak, in psychological soil. The more happily born child has the chance for slow, healthy growth into vigorous maturity. Biologically and psychologically he may be inferior to the child of the migrant worker. But precisely as the best seed in the world cannot grow well in poor soil, so the high capabilities of the migrant child are little likely to develop in an environment that is deadly to the human spirit.

Democracy's task, then, is to find out how to equalize the soil conditions of life. It must give to all its people equal opportunity to grow.

## II

When we think of equality in this way, many of the things we have been doing in the past few decades gain significance. Take such a simple thing as public education. The task of equalizing educational advantages is as yet far from having been achieved. School opportunities in a poverty-stricken area are worlds removed from those that are available in more prosperous regions. Nevertheless, even when they are poor, these opportunities bring into sharp relief what democracy *intends.* Education is something everybody needs. Some day democracy intends that everybody shall get the full education he needs.

Many things, however, will have to be done before this is achieved, for education depends not merely upon the school. It also depends upon home conditions. School conditions may be equalized, as they are in many of our large cities; but where home conditions are glaringly unequal, there is unequal opportunity for growth. Such glaring inequalities of home conditions again trace back most frequently to inequalities of income. Efforts to equalize education must, therefore, carry with them efforts to overcome gross inequalities of income. Equalization of income, however, requires the removal of the power of some to depress the living standards of others. Thus, it is obvious that efforts to equalize educational opportunities require efforts to achieve more just economic arrangements.

This is one long job ahead of us. It is perhaps the central job of our civilization; and it is not likely that we shall complete it for decades to come. However, there is a way of approaching the task which promises speedier success. When we think of income inequality we tend to think of it merely in money-terms. But we have learned ingenious ways of increasing incomes that are not money-ways at all. Take the aforesaid matter of education. The actual amount of service and equipment that has been at the command of the average student who has graduated from high school, if bought by him personally, would mount into amazing figures. During his years of schooling, he has had about two score teachers at his service, besides a costly equipment of buildings, school furniture, laboratories, and library. Had he been required to buy even the part-time services of the teachers and the necessary part of this equipment, he would have had to be a wealthy boy. But he is a poor boy, living on a meager farm which yields an income of only a few hundred dollars. Nevertheless, by what looks like a social miracle, he is given services and use of equipment which even a wealthy boy could not buy.

It is a simple idea that need not be elaborated; but it is easily forgotten. All public services and properties are part of the actual income of the users. Thus the greater amount of public services and properties we have at our disposal, the greater our income. Every road we drive on, every park we enjoy, every service we use—of post office or police or fire department—

increases such income. We are given these services and properties for a relatively small tax. Here, again, is something that looks like a social miracle: each individual, by contributing a little, secures for himself hundreds and thousands of times more than he could otherwise secure for himself.

Here, then, is one clear way toward the equalizing of incomes: namely, by devising public services that are good for everybody and that could not possibly be secured each for himself. Those of us who are interested in the equalizing of opportunities must therefore learn to be keen about the multiplication of such public services. They are not—as is sometimes asserted—a means of pauperizing people. Have public schools pauperized? Parks? Libraries? Post offices? Nor are they a means of introducing regimentation. They are simply one intelligent way of enabling all of us to get for ourselves what no one of us could get for himself. Rather than resist these, we should be eager to extend all the wise forms of public services and public properties.

## III

Another method of equalizing in which a democracy must be interested is the establishment of what might be called "an irreducible minimum." There are levels of life below which people must not be permitted to fall. Among us, for example, are millions of "shrunken bellies." Obviously, this is not a happy circumstance for the victims. But also it is not good for the rest of us, for it breeds in us an insensitivity to life frustration. Increasingly, a democratic people evince their democratic sincerity by being solicitous about the many who have a less than living income; whose work is seasonal, insecure, and badly paid; whose diet is below the nourishment level; and whose housing is below the decency level. We have begun to recognize our responsibility to the unemployed by giving them a basic support. We do this because they are the victims of economic tragedy beyond their control. We have still, however, to learn our responsibility to those who are the victims of a system that creates the migrant worker, the sharecropper, the tenant farmer, the seasonal worker. These people, too, are not personally to blame. While many of them are, indeed, shiftless and unintelligent, most of them are caught in an imperfect system. We have to devise means of guaranteed support whereby such victims may be kept from falling below an irreducible minimum. Only those who are completely insensitive to suffering and ignorant of its causes in an economic system that has got out of hand will call this pauperization.

## IV

One of the chief obstacles, however, to democratic equality is the presence among us of a new form of special privilege. Long ago we revolted against feudal privilege and established freedom of enterprise as our peculiar American right. Much water, however, has run under the bridge since then. We need to realize that another kind of privilege has grown up among us. In many ways it is the twentieth-century counterpart of the feudalism we repudiated in the eighteenth.

This new type of privilege is peculiarly and exasperatingly undemocratic. Democracy purposes to be a relation of equality among men—equality as to essential power. This is expressed in political form by the phrase, "one man one vote." Each man, in basic voting power, is to count for one and no more than one. If a man manages to count as more than one, it is because surreptitiously he has bought up the suffrage power of other men. By such surreptitious purchase he has changed himself into a multiple man. Democracy can allow no such multiple men. England found that out in her "rotten boroughs." We have found it out in the various corruptions of our politics. Democracy can permit no multiple men for the simple reason that it fails just as soon as it permits a preponderance of power to be concentrated in one man or group of men.

However, economic enterprise of the kind that has grown up among us makes multiple men. Its basic relationship is expressed not by the phrase, "one man one vote," but by the phrase, "one share one vote." In capitalistic enterprise one man may, by his ownership of many shares, achieve the strength of many. With this strength of many, he is able to control the destiny of many. He becomes their source of livelihood, masters their movements, commands their hours and days, makes or breaks their happiness. To control men in these ways means to govern them.

Thus a new and perilous factor has entered democracy. A man with the strength of millions has more power to shape the destiny of his fellows than a man with merely the strength of one vote. The millionfold man, then, becomes to that extent the ruler of his fellows. Rulership gets transferred from the political field to the economic. Democracy is thereby changed into a kind of near-plutocracy. The "consent of the governed" becomes the submission of the governed to the power of ownership. To the extent that economic might rules men's lives, democracy disappears.

This is the transformation that America has, in large measure, undergone. Ostensibly still a political democracy, it has come dangerously near to being an economic oligarchy. In many basic ways Americans are now ruled by money-power. They are ruled not by men and women who stand relatively equal in strength, but by men and women who are multiplied many times by the influence of their wealth.

How did this happen? The simple answer is it happened because we passed out of man-to-man capitalism—the capitalism of the small owner and the small partnership—into corporation-capitalism; from the capitalism of the direct owner, who could see and handle his property, to the capitalism of the absentee owner, who knows his property in the form of paper certificates. The early kind of capitalism—man-to-man, direct-ownership capitalism—was relatively safe for democracy, for it led to no great inequalities of power. On the other hand, this later form of capitalism—corporation-absentee-ownership capitalism (sometimes called finance-capitalism)—constitutes one of democracy's gravest dangers, because in it power is so piled on power that the common man is lost under the hugeness of it. This passage from earlier, man-to-man capitalism to corporation-capitalism marks one of the greatest, though still largely unrecognized, revolutions of our time. "It is of the essence of revolutions of the more silent sort that they are unrecognized until they are far advanced. This was the case with the so-called Industrial Revolution and is the case with the corporate revolution through which we are at present passing. The transfer of perhaps two-thirds of the industrial wealth of the country from individual ownership to ownership by large, publicly financed corporations vitally changes the lives of property owners, the lives of workers, and the methods of property tenure." [1]

As worker, consumer, and citizen, the American is under the command of corporate powers that he is largely impotent through his individual effort to mitigate or control. We realize gratefully, of course, that we in America are far freer, as individuals, than Germans, Poles, Czechs, Italians, Japanese, and present-day French. This, however, is hardly to the point. The grave question we are now confronting is whether there has not entered into our way of life a power that is a threat to democratic equality. As we look forward to the further development of our nation, must we not seek to curb the unhealthy growth of this form of corporate might which goes counter to the basic man-to-man equality which is of the essence of democracy?

## V

There are at least three ways in which we can curb this undue growth. One is the way of building up

[1] A. A. Berle and G. C. Means, *The Modern Corporation and Private Property* (New York: Macmillan & Co., 1934).

counterpower. Herein lies the democratic significance of the labor movement. It is obvious to us now that the individual worker is as nothing compared with the strength of the corporation for which he works. He "takes it or leaves it." The only way in which he can have any say as to the treatment he is to receive is by multiplying his strength through association with his fellows. Collective bargaining, in short, must be one of democracy's ways of saving the worker from complete subjection to corporate power.

We may set it down as a democratic axiom, therefore, that as long as, in capitalistic enterprise, the power of a single individual or group may be multiplied many times by the ownership of shares, the power of the single worker must be multiplied many times by organized association with fellow workers.

A second way of meeting the undue growth of economic power is by regulatory laws that check its abuses. The last few years have witnessed the enactment of many such laws: laws governing the operation of the security market, protecting depositors against bank failures, regulating the formation of holding companies, and protecting mortgagees. Granted the continuance of the system of free enterprise (the substitution of a sheer state capitalism or of a communistic collectivism seems wholly out of the American picture), the preservation of democracy will require a vigilant policy of regulation to protect democratic right against the encroachment of economic might.

A third way of meeting the undue growth of economic power is by the extension of a form of economic enterprise–consumers' co-operation–which, surprisingly enough, retains the democratic principle of "one man one vote." In this form of business enterprise no greater power is lodged in the owner of a hundred shares than in the owner of one. Thus, no matter how large the ownership, voting power remains equal among all the owners.

This has constituted the democratic strength of the co-operative movement. Whether a co-operative commonwealth will displace the present mixture of political democracy and economic plutocracy, we do not know. But, judging from the experience of such nations as Denmark and Sweden, it may be safely asserted that a wide extension of this highly democratic form of economic enterprise will not only be good in itself, but will be a powerful check upon many of the abuses of our present capitalistic system.

This, in addition, needs to be said about the importance of the co-operative movement. As a maker of democratic equality, it differs psychologically from the methods of collective bargaining and legal regulation. Both of these are, in essence, methods to be used to secure one portion of our population *against* the activities of another portion. They are profoundly necessary methods in the present imperfect state of our society. But to some extent, at least, both are necessary evils. As long-range techniques for effecting democratic justice, they both have their drawbacks.

Because collective bargaining is a "fight" technique that has grown up in response to an exploitative technique, it inevitably tends to slice our society along class and economic lines, into self-conscious and mutually antagonistic groups. Such differences of opinion among the people of our democracy as have traditionally been represented by political party lines have never really threatened our essential oneness; for our party lines, historically, have been perpendicular lines cutting through our society from top to bottom: we have had rich Republicans, and poor and middle class; rich Democrats, and poor and middle class; rural Republicans and urban; rural Democrats and urban. But when the cleavage is a horizontal one along class lines—as it increasingly threatens to become in America—we begin to have all the people conditioned by one sort of background and one set of loyalties on one side, and all those conditioned by another sort of background and another set of loyalties on the other side. It is, then, hard to find words with which either side can talk across the chasm, because there are not enough common experiences to tap as bases of common understanding. Once this sort of line-up becomes the dominant one in a society, the essential unity of that society is threatened. Pressure against pressure holds a society in too precarious a balance to be safe. Collective bargaining, then, is necessary as long as financial and industrial powers are so organized in their collective might that the individual worker is helpless against them; but while the method safeguards democracy on one front, it may very well threaten it on another front. If it is to be both useful and safe, this method of equality making has to be tempered by others that bridge the gap.

A similar criticism can be made of regulatory laws. They are laws to *prevent* certain types of behavior. They are necessary. No doubt about that. But they are not good enough, for they work from the top down. While they may, indeed, in the long run, build such new social habits and expectations that old exploitative ways will seem intolerable to the heirs of those who once used them, this educational function is incidental to the preventative function. And as mere preventers, any laws tend to range group against group.

The co-operative method differs from both of these in three profound respects. First, since all of us are consumers, it cuts across economic lines and brings together people of different classes and vocations who would not be brought together by the haphazard incidents of our usual economy. Second, it deals with people not only in their capacity as makers and sellers of goods, but in their capacity as users of goods. Hence it tends to cultivate the tastes and discrimination of people and to make them more mentally and emotionally fit for the world of high production to which we are making our awkward adjustment. Third, as has often been pointed out, co-operation is democracy from the bottom up. It safeguards people by making them more informed about economic processes and more capable of handling these, rather than by building around them a protective wall of laws that safeguards them whether or not they know what is going on.

There are obvious limits to how far the antagonistic pressures of organized business and organized labor can go without cutting our democracy into two irreconcilable camps. There are obvious limits to how far government regulation can go within a democratic framework. But the method of co-operation, being not only an economic device, but an educational and psychological one for helping people to get an intimate understanding of their society and a skill in working well with other people, is capable of indefinite expansion. As a long-range method, then, it is perhaps the most democratic technique available for increasing not only equality of resources, but equality of understanding.

Economic privilege, as it has developed in America,

is a serious threat to democracy. But with vigilance and wisdom we can meet it—not by the drastic method of casting out the system which creates it, but by checking its abuses. At the same time, as in the case of the cooperative movement, we can be free to make experiments in other forms of enterprise which seem more truly to embody the method and spirit of democracy.

This way, of vigilant regulation and of trying out new experiments, would seem to be democracy's way of slow growth toward a more acceptable system of enterprise. Democracy will do ill to adopt the method of dictatorial overthrow—whether the overthrow be in the interest of the capitalistic possessors of wealth or of the proletarian nonpossessors.

## VI

We have spoken of five ways of achieving equality of opportunity. All of them fall within the fairly well-recognized pattern of our society. There is a sixth way, however, which is not as widely recognized. It is a way that is more specifically related to the kind of technological order which we have been developing during the last few decades.

This is an age of machine production. In one sense machine production has brought to us a new and deeply disturbing problem, namely, that of technological unemployment. Machines displace men. Since there is no chance that we shall go back to premachine industry, the problem of labor displacement becomes a crucial one. Many persons stop with the problem and go no further. One frequently hears it said that since increasing mechanical efficiency means increasing labor displacement, we must look forward to an army—perhaps an increasing army—of permanently unemployed; for no one seems able to show us how displaced workers can be replaced in a machine economy that does not need them.

However, one crucial point is usually overlooked. Machine production in America has thus far been geared not to mass consumption but to class consumption. Think of automobile production. We call it mass production, because we *produce* in mass. But who buys the automobiles that come off the assembly line? Certainly not the people who are living on a small weekly wage—twenty-five dollars a week or less. Automobiles are still being produced for a high-level middle class. Might they be produced for mass consumption? Engineering experts have been telling us for years that far cheaper (and equally sturdy) automobiles could be produced if the automobile industry were mass-consumption minded and set its engineering intelligence to work to produce for the low-income level of millions of our population.

The same is true of practically all the products of our machine economy. "Advertising has addressed its appeal frankly to the few who can afford a hand-tailored, preindustrial exclusiveness. But in an era of machines is it exactly sensible to design so many things, all needed, so that the man of average income can secure one of them only by foregoing most of his other normal needs? . . . No one today bothers to ask how much the $25 a week average consumer should pay out on a new refrigerator selling for $160, plus usurious interest, when one suited to its job can be designed for him . . . at a factory cost of $30. No one asks what proportion of his affluence this average consumer should pay, plus carrying charges, for a de luxe electric range at $149, a bedroom suite at $139, a washing machine at $79, a motor car that has no value, parked, at $799, or an unfurnished house at $4,999, plus . . .

"Here, ten years after our inherited culture began to crumble at its foundations, we still are refusing to consider existing levels of income in the design of our major necessities. . . . We simply refuse to face the fact that the inability of two-thirds of our population to enjoy the fruits of a machine economy, except piecemeal and at secondhand, is largely unimaginative design." [2]

[2] Corwin Willson, "Designing the National Defense Program," *Dynamic America*, January, 1941.

Suppose we should capture this new idea, that a machine economy can, if it will, address its engineering intelligence to production for mass consumption of all the major products of that economy. What would this mean? It would mean that the income level of millions of people would be stepped up, that they would have access to products which make for decency and convenience in life; in short, that they would have a living standard which is now utterly beyond them.

As the writer above quoted goes on to say: "To keep machines busy, we are beginning to suspect, requires a different *kind* of thinking than was adequate to keep a slow-tempo handicraft economy muddling through. Handicraft thinking was aristocratic, and aristocratic thinking was and remains preponderately political in character. An example is the faith of many preindustrially-minded persons in our ability to legislate an increase in mass purchasing power. . . . Eventually we may become adult enough to realize . . . that the easiest way to spread mass purchasing power, i. e. proportion it, is by re-design."

This is an idea about equalizing opportunities that is only just beginning to filter through into our consciousness. We still, for the most part, think preindustrially and hope that by preindustrial legislative devices we may turn the trick of making a class-geared industrial system serve our needs for wider distribution. But such legislation simply will not work. As long as our industrial system is not mass conscious, as long as it remains a class-production system, the problem of technological unemployment and of a generally low standard of living must forever remain unsolved. Once, however, we realize the possibility of a productive system geared to mass consumption, we put ourselves not only on the way to solving the problem of technological unemployment but to lifting the general standard of living throughout America. The invitation that our industrial system issues to all of us is to stop thinking preindustrially and to think industrially. Our machines, if given the chance, can be of powerful help in bringing increased opportunities for life and happiness to vast numbers of our population. Instead of continuing to enslave the masses and indulge the classes, they may yet serve to liberate millions of Americans who have never been liberated before.

We have seen that there are six basic ways of equalizing opportunities: (1) through a raising of income levels by the extension of public services; (2) through the guaranty of an irreducible minimum; (3) through the regulatory checking of the abuses of economic privilege; (4) through collective bargaining; (5) through consumers' co-operation; and (6) through a mass-consumption economy. The many-sidedness of this program is not its weakness but its strength. It indicates that whatever other mistakes we shall make, we shall not make the easy one of oversimplifying our problem.

We are far from having reached the stage at which we can say, "Lo, this is the solution." Democracy has been called "a many-headed monster." It should rather be called a many-headed experiment. As soon as it becomes single-headed—with the "truth" dictated from above—it then becomes a monster. For among us imperfect humans there is no single political and economic truth that once and for all can make us equal in our basic human rights. We accept such a "truth" at our peril. Whether we like it or not, we must live out our human destiny of having to move, by trial and error, and by successive wisdom, toward an increasing and many-sided removal of the inequalities that hamper and restrict our lives.

## ★ *16* ★

# NEW DESIGNS FOR INDIVIDUALITY

## I

THERE are two ways in which we human beings can fall short of being personalities: one is to remain starkly separate individuals—so starkly separate that the traits which we can develop only by group linkages are left dormant. The other is to become crowd-individuals—so merged in the mass that we have significance only as units to be counted, not as personalities that can leave distinguishing marks upon our environments.

Our economic life in America has tended, all too largely, to create these two types of subpersonalities. On the one hand, the driving absorption of our economic interests has tended to separate us into individuals, each striving for his own advancement. We have praised competition as the life of trade. No doubt our praise has, to an extent, been justified. But we have failed to see that competition, too relentlessly pursued, may come near to being the death of personality. We are becoming a nation of big cities and bedroom suburbs, where individuals move as strangers, each tenaciously—and precariously—hanging on to his own advantage. What looks like strength in us is, in deeper reality, fear: fear of one another—of the competitor on the job, the competitor in sales, the competitor in social prestige; fear of the system which may suddenly turn upon us and leave us destitute.

> We dive, each man, into his secret house,
> And bolt the door, and listen in affright,
> Each timid man beside a timid spouse,
> With timid children huddled out of sight.[1]

It is not a pretty picture. We have romanticized ourselves as a sturdy people; but we have failed to see that a sturdy people must be a warm and understanding people. Being solely interested in our own affairs is not good enough for American democracy.

## II

While economic interest has thus separated many of us into competing individuals, economic processes have pulverized others of us into the anonymity of crowd-individuals. Mass production is no respecter of per-

[1] James Stephens, "The Road," from *Songs from the Clay* (New York: Macmillan & Co.).

sonality. The man who endlessly turns nut 341 is hardly, through that process, permitted to attain the stature of a significant individual. Nor is the man or the woman who endlessly picks cotton—or grapes, or hops, or peaches—at next to nothing a day, who moves from area to area, voteless and homeless, helped to the attainment of a rich and responsible personality. These people are symptomatic of what is happening in America. Mass production—whether in factories or fields—has been leveling people down, so that, in vast numbers, they have become even less than individuals. They have been made into robots.

To be sure, some of these robots have enough courage and vitality to organize in their own defense. To this extent—aside from their contribution of work—they are significant for our civilization. Democracy requires that oppression be opposed. These workers, therefore, achieve a certain stature of manhood and womanhood by the courage and intelligence of their opposition.

But this achievement is not enough. To be occupied chiefly in doing two things—endlessly repeating a task that is neither respected nor loved, and joining forces against economic oppression—is not sufficient to build the kind of personality that a democracy needs. There can be no joy in contemplating the millions of factory robots, behind-the-counter robots, sharecroppers, migrant workers, tenant farmers that make up a large part of our population. Neither can there be joy in contemplating the millions of small businessmen, endlessly jealous of one another and of the big businessmen, and of the thousands of big businessmen endlessly seeking to put it over on other big businessmen and on the small businessmen.

Can we pull ourselves out of this spiritual poverty? This is the question which is paramount for the America of the future. Can we raise the level of manhood and womanhood? Or, as mass production and mass competition increase, must personality among us decrease?

## III

Two things are necessary for personality—love of work and love of fellow men. This need not be argued. The wisdom of all the ages comes to this, that human beings are at their best when they can surrender themselves to work they care about and human beings they care about. A democracy, then, that is solicitous about the quality of the manhood and womanhood of its citizens, will strive for this: for a people that love their work and care about their fellows.

Viewing the highly competitive, mass-production life we live, with its pulverization of our nation into millions of self-interested individuals, it seems an impossible thing to hope for. Revolutionary thinkers tell us that it cannot be achieved save at the cost of a complete overthrow of our present system of competitive enterprise. They may be right; but more likely they are wrong. To attempt to achieve a better order of life by a complete overthrow of our present order is at best an impatient way of going at things; and we seem always to find that this impatient way brings more evils than it banishes. However, what is chiefly wrong about this view is that, in aiming to improve democracy, it seeks to dispense with it altogether. It seeks to *compel* a whole class of recalcitrant people to adhere to a projected new order of things. Disbelieving in the slow ways of persuasion and growth, it looks for a short cut to Utopia, and plans its short cut by slashing through the bodies and souls of the still unconvinced.

There must be a better way than this. We show ourselves to have little faith in our fellow men if, after a hundred and sixty odd years of fairly successful democratic experience, we decide now that the iron way of compulsion is the only way of achieving the more humanized society we desire. What we should thereby achieve would probably be not a more humanized society, but one dehumanized by hates and resistances.

To develop a nation in which people love their work and their fellow men seems not a great deal to ask. In fact, from the point of view of the Christianity we have professed, it seems the quite necessary thing to ask. For to be willing partners in the perpetuation of conditions that make for widespread hatred of work and unconcern about one's fellows is hardly to "be about (our) Father's business."

American economic life, it would seem, must Christianize itself to the extent at least that it becomes serious enough about the damage it has been doing to people as people to cease doing the damage. As a nation, we cannot continue much longer in the way we are going. We talk proudly of government of, by, and for the people. It would sound very different if we were to talk of government of, by, and for mass-production slaves and mass-production enslavers. The statement, of course, is oversimplified. But it is true enough to make us feel uneasy.

## IV

So we come to grips with our question: how can we begin to move toward an order of life in which there is widespread love of work and love of fellow men?

It is a question that must first be asked by people who have some margin of choice in the conduct of their life. By these I mean employers, and professional men and women.

One thing that our educational system has never yet done is to give individuals a clear sense of the social implications of their vocations. The reason for this is obvious. It goes back to what we said in Chapter 13: education for societal understanding has hitherto been reserved for juveniles. Inasmuch as juveniles are not yet engaged in vocations, they cannot be led to think intelligently about the social implications of a specific vocation. Such thinking can be done only when the vocation has become a central interest in the life of the individual. To be sure, youngsters are given some general information about the social values of the several vocations, but since their interest is not yet specifically engaged, such information comes to them, at best, as only vague generalizations.

Here, then, is another reason for specific and disciplined education in the adult years. The individual is now bending his energies in pursuit of a vocation. He is at the point where he is intensely interested in making good. Psychologically, he is ripe for viewing his vocation in all its human relationships. This is the time, then, when he should be given the chance to do more than learn the skills required. He should also be given the chance to learn how his vocation fits into the wide scheme of human relationships.

The lawyer needs this. Sometimes he gets a little of it in the law-school years. But for the most part he is there learning law-skills. When he is actively in practice, however, he is in vivid contact with the human situation. Questions about the relation of law to social welfare come to his mind which, in his individual way, he seeks to answer. Perhaps he does and perhaps he does not answer them. Cases press for attention; he has to make his living. He is offered no companionship in the solving of these broader issues. There is no place to which he can go, no association of similarly trained minds which he can join to help him toward a broad human view of his profession. Bar Associations help a little but not much. They seem mainly to be defensive organizations, formed to uphold the honor and the perquisites of the profession.

In one of our Midwestern cities, a wise Catholic bishop has organized a lawyer group. These men meet together at stated intervals to discuss the social obligations of their profession. Here is a beginning: adult minds seeking in an adult way to understand the broad human implications of their lifework. We need such lawyer groups by the hundreds and thousands. For the psychological effect of such group-exploration is to make the individual lawyer more vividly aware of his human relations. As these wider realities engage his mind, he becomes a personality more competent to serve in a democracy.

Physicians need this. One of the puzzling facts in

recent years has been the stubborn refusal of great numbers of physicians to be interested in any departure from the old ways of competitive medicine. Undoubtedly, the problems involved in the socializing of medicine are many and perplexing; but they are problems that will have to be solved. Physicians, by and large, exhibit an immaturity of societal thinking. They are excellent and devoted specialists; but the educational system in which they have had their training has not helped them to broad societal outlooks. In a profession that is profoundly social in its bearings, they have remained in large measure isolated individualists.

There are, of course, many physicians who, by the grace of their social passion, have become more than individualized specialists, but they have to meet the stubborn resistance of the societally immature. There is only one way out of this: medicine must envisage an education for its members that will go on after they have begun their practice. Such education should concern itself with more than the refining of specific skills. It should call for disciplined and searching thought about the social implications of the profession.

Businessmen need this. It is heartening to find that businessmen are beginning to talk of business as a "profession." A profession is characterized by two things: a recognized standard of preparation and a sense of social obligation. If and when business becomes a profession and not merely a struggle for individual income making, we may expect that the social obligations of business will be increasingly made evident. Small beginnings of this new consciousness are found in the pronouncements of various business and industrial organizations. But pronouncements by a governing board, or by some committee of members, are not enough. Too often they are platitudinous generalizations that serve only as a front to conceal practices that are not so good. What is profoundly needed among business people is prolonged and disciplined thinking about the social implications of their pursuits. Industrialists cannot much longer turn their consciences away from the damage which mass-production methods do to the minds and souls of workers. Nor can financiers much longer remain unaware of the demoralizing effects upon all classes of people of the various processes of financial thimblerigging. All business, industrial, and financial pursuits are due for an overhauling in the minds of those who pursue them.

This means that businessmen and women—like lawyers, physicians, teachers, artists, advertisers—need to put their adult heads together to find out what it is they are doing and what the effects of their doings are upon the common human welfare.

This is one way in which individuals can be made into more than individualists. As such broadening and enriching of personality takes place among our specialists, we may confidently expect that not only social understanding but social good will will increase.

After all, the old knightly dictum, *noblesse oblige*, should still hold. Those who have had the good fortune to rise higher in life than the rest have the obligation to use their good fortune in behalf of their less lucky fellows. We remember Goldsmith's lines:

> Ill fares the land, to hastening ills a prey,
> Where wealth accumulates, and men decay.

But where men and women who have achieved—wealth, prestige, power—give the honest energy of their minds to finding out how they can help others to achieve, we need not fear the hastening ills.

However, it is later than we think. An immense amount of damage—to ourselves as personalities, and to our less happily circumstanced fellows—has already been done. We shall need, quickly, to find ways in which we adults, in our several vocations, can limber up our minds and take stock of the things we ought to be doing and ought to cease doing.

## V

Perhaps this is enough for a beginning. But there are millions of unconsidered people, and they will have to do something about themselves. Democracy is a system of self-government. We can never hope to achieve the full enrichment of our democratic life by having the fortunate ones do the thinking and the acting for the less fortunate. To repeat a quotation already used, "Free men set themselves free." The "robots," if such they are, must de-robotize themselves.

In scores of ways this is already being done. While the story of the labor struggle is deeply significant, the story of the struggle of workers to educate themselves is perhaps more so. A good deal of this education, indeed, has been gained through the picket line, through negotiations with employers, through the organization of a strong and intelligent preparedness. The individual worker who has learned that he must not, even at large pay, take the job of a striking fellow worker, has to that extent achieved a deepening and broadening of his personality. He refuses to be a lone wolf. He is a *fellow* worker. He has learned the lesson of each for all and all for each. Because workers have been learning this lesson now for a number of generations, it is not surprising that there is among them, in general, a broader and more enlightened social sense than one often finds among men and women of property and privilege.

It needs to be remembered that it was working people who did most to establish the public-school system.

It is significant that today, when privileged interests are using the excuse of a war crisis to strike at education, it is the workers who are united in education's defense.

American workers have not yet been entirely robotized. They do many foolish things, such as their present foolish division among themselves. But of them it may be said that their basic aim is identical with that of democracy: namely, to build a land where equality of opportunity to be persons in their own right is achieved for all.

Workers have long realized that they must educate themselves. They have realized, too, that education through conflict is not enough. They know that there must be education through understanding and through enriched experience. They have set themselves about the task of giving themselves this education.

The most significant thing about the various types of workers' education that have quietly grown up in our midst is that they are forms of adult education. Workers are not so naïve as to believe that the lessons they were taught in the schools provide them with enough wisdom for their adult life. They go to their workers' schools precisely because they know that the juvenile schools never taught—never could teach—them the things they now, in their working life, need to know.

Workers' education has had hard sledding in America—far more so than in England and the Scandinavian countries. But it is now definitely on the map. Nor is it education that merely concerns itself with the conflicts of employers and employees. Increasingly workers are demanding for themselves the kind of education that gives not only understanding of social problems, but richness of personal experience. In short, workers, denied by their working conditions the privilege of being persons in their own right, have, for a number of decades, been taking the matter into their own hands, and, through their own self-constituted classes, have been making themselves persons in their own right.

This is the most hopeful thing that is happening among workers. The more radical among them would say that they are preparing themselves to be intelligent enough to take over when the old system goes bankrupt. The more moderate would say that they are preparing themselves to live as intelligent and resourceful individuals in a democracy that asks its citizens to be intelligent and resourceful.

America needs people—people who care about their work and care about other people. The frenzied individualism that has characterized the young years of our national life will have to change into something more mature, more wisely geared to our democratic beliefs. The time is at hand when prosperity-building will have to transform itself into personality-building as well. For a democracy, however prosperous in dollars, fails if it is not equally prosperous in the quality of its individuals.

Adults—whether privileged or underprivileged—have the task today of making this land into one in which people respect their work and care about their fellows. This is the gravest task we now have to undertake. It cannot be undertaken unless we all—privileged and underprivileged alike—do honest and disciplined thinking about the social implications of our jobs. This very confronting of ourselves will be the beginning of a new social wisdom and of a new quality in our personality.

## * 17 *

# NEW DESIGNS FOR THE COMMUNITY

## I

AMERICA began as a face-to-face democracy. People came together and threshed out their problems in town meetings. Everybody took part. "In a town meeting," said Emerson in his Concord address, "the great secret of political science was uncovered, and the problem solved, how to give every individual his fair weight. . . . In a town meeting the roots of society were reached. Here the rich gave counsel, but the poor also; and, moreover, the just and the unjust. In this open democracy, every opinion had utterance; every objection, every fact, every acre of land, every bushel of rye, its entire weight." And he went on to say, "It is the consequence of this institution that not a schoolhouse, a public pew, a bridge, a pound, a mill-dam, hath been set up, or pulled down, or altered, or bought, or sold, without the whole population of this town having a voice in the affair. A general contentment is the result. And the people truly feel that they are lords of the soil. In every winding road, in every stone fence, in the smokes of the poorhouse chimney, in the clock on the church, they read their own power, and consider, at leisure, the wisdom and error of their judgments."

The America of face-to-face democracy no longer exists—or exists only in a few small villages. In town, city, state, and nation our democracy may be more aptly described as impersonal, as democracy by paper symbols, democracy by distant delegation. Instead of being the face-to-face relationship of neighbors, it is the going-in-all-directions relationship of strangers. American democracy is now in the period of the Great Dispersion.

In those face-to-face days "a general contentment" was the result. People felt that they were "lords of the soil." In these going-in-all-directions days there is, on the contrary, a general uneasiness, a sense of not belonging, of being out of things. Citizens feel that they are largely unconsidered digits in an impersonal spread of politics and business. Public opinion takes vague shape somehow—mysteriously, anonymously. It is the amorphous product of radio listening, newspaper reading, lecture hearing, stray comments in passing, the wisdom and wisecracks of columnists, night-club chatter. The individual citizen has no way of feeling that he, as an individual, can have a hand in *creating* public opinion. I remember the pathetic delight of the wife of a Midwestern college president who announced to the assembled company that she had at last been interviewed by the Gallup Poll. For the first time she had counted as somebody!

To be strangers in a strange land can be a pleasant experience when we are traveling through. Then we are on a holiday, irresponsible. It is not our own land, and we have nothing to do about it. But to be strangers in our own land is different. We have to do something about our own land. It asks us to be useful citizens. But in the vast impersonality of things how can we be useful?

Town-meeting democracy caused the individual to broaden his interests to take in the whole community. He did not have to be jammed within the narrowness of his private affairs. There were things for him to think about that had to do with the common good. John Stuart Mill saw what the town-meeting process did to the moral outlook of the individual: "He must weigh interests not his own; must be guided by another rule than his private partialities; must look out for the general good, the public interests." [1]

[1] Quoted in *Old South Leaflets: The Town Meeting* (Boston: Old South Meeting House, 1883), p. 6.

In those days, in short, people were given a natural opportunity to become public-minded. It is different today. We of the present generation, because there is no easily available way of participating in public affairs, are turned back to the cultivation of our private affairs. Indeed, it has become a habit of our day to say to people: "Your best contribution to the public good is to do well the particular job you are doing. If you are a businessman, be a good businessman. If you are a teacher, be a good teacher." Or, to use the evangelistic phrase, we say: "Brighten the corner where you are. God will take care of the rest."

We scarcely realize it, but there is here a kind of counsel of despair. Being unable to give to ourselves, through direct, face-to-face participation, the broadening of mind that comes through an active caring about community interests, we turn to our private affairs and hope that through an intense and honest preoccupation with them we can do our bit for our country.

But the adding together of private preoccupations does not sum up to a public-minded people. It sums up to just so many millions of private-minded people.

And this, in large measure, is America today: an aggregate of private-minded people.

## II

Freedom is powerful in its unifying effects when freedom involves an active participation in public concerns. Freedom, however, can be powerfully disunifying when it involves solely preoccupation with our private concerns. The grave problem of American democracy—since we cannot return to the early town-meeting way of life—is to discover some new way of direct participation in the creation of public good.

Some Americans have been discovering this new way. If all of us could discover it, we should cease being a democracy of paper symbols and distant delegation, and should once more become one of face-to-face participation.

To understand this new discovery, we must consider first what has happened to the town meeting of blessed memory. We might draw a small circle and place within it the word "town meeting." Within that small circle all the affairs of the community were carried on—community planning, community building, education, religion, recreation, charity. They could all be carried on by everybody because the community was small and its affairs were few. Since then the community has grown large and its affairs have multiplied. As they have multiplied they have been taken over by special groups within the community. We might represent this by lines radiating out from the small circle into wedge-shaped areas. Thus education has come to be a function organized and directed by independent groups of people: school boards, parent-teachers associations, school faculties. Help to the unfortunate has likewise come to be organized and directed by independent groups: community fund committees, charitable societies, public health boards, staffs of social settlements. The small town-meeting circle of activities, in short, has not disappeared; it has merely divided and extended itself into functions performed by various bodies of people within the community.

Let us list some of these public functions:

1. Social-service Functions. These include all the agencies and activities that are directed toward the amelioration of suffering, of loneliness, of personal defeat in a community. Charity organization societies and visiting nurses' associations serve this purpose; so does a welfare council; so does a social settlement or a public employment bureau.

2. Watchdog Functions. The old town meeting was a perfect place for the exercise of the eternal vigilance necessary for a democracy. This function is now being performed by various associations such as nonpartisan leagues, the League of Women Voters, citizens' unions.

3. Policy-forming Functions. These are now being

performed, at least in their first necessary stages, by the coming together of citizens in groups to discuss their common problems: public forums, discussion groups, Town Meeting of the Air, People's Forum, Foreign Policy Association, Chicago Round Table, policy-making groups among business and professional men and women.

4. Community-planning Functions. These are being performed by various bodies of citizens who sit on commissions to plan the future of their communities. Architects, engineers, educators, public-minded businessmen devote their specialized skills to the consideration of the ways in which communities may extend their facilities and prevent the unsightly mushroom growths that have been characteristic of the past decades.

5. Educational Functions. These are performed not only by elective boards of education, but by parent-teachers associations, teachers' professional societies, adult education councils.

6. Recreative Functions. These are not only performed by delegated authorities in a community, but also by voluntary groups of citizens interested in furthering wholesome recreational activities. Here, too, are to be listed Y.M.'s and Y.W.'s, social settlements; also folk dance groups, committees for public dance

halls, groups that review and evaluate moving pictures, radio advisory committees.

7. Religious Functions. These—in their wider public relationship—are performed by interdenominational ministers' associations, Friends Service Committees, forum committees in churches, Good Will Committees, conferences of Jews and Christians.

## III

When we look at the situation in this way, America suddenly comes alive. Not only are hundreds of thousands of people doing things of a public nature, but countless opportunities are open to millions of our people to do these things. The neighborliness of the town meeting is indeed gone; but a new kind of neighborliness is now possible. It is the neighborliness of direct participation in some area of public usefulness.

The means, then, are at hand. The only problem, now, is to get Americans to use these means.

At present, we seem to be in a transition stage. We have left the old, all-embracing neighborliness behind; but we have not as yet achieved the new kind of neighborliness that is now possible. Most Americans are still outside the picture we have drawn. Most of them are private individuals confined within the limits of their private affairs. The problem is to get these private-minded people to come out of the small areas of their self-concern and be active in at least one area of public concern.

How far we still are from this is made clear by a community survey conducted by the Adult Education Department of the University of Michigan. The survey was undertaken to test out the truth or falsity of an oft-repeated statement that is made by people whenever a new venture—like a forum or a community council—is proposed. The typical reaction to the suggestion is a wearied look on the faces of the "prominent" citizens and the assertion that no new project can be undertaken in that particular community because "people are already going to too many things, are belonging to too many associations."

"A common exercise on the part of those engrossed in community activities is to rehearse with evident pride a long list of community enterprises. The implication is that the town already has a formidable array of achievements to its credit. When some doubt is expressed a roar goes up to the effect that the town is already over-organized and that anything new would be excessive. The most common statement employed to express this attitude is, 'It is almost impossible to find a night in the week when something isn't going on. This is the most over-organized town in this part of the state.' This kind of talk betrays how far the community 'busybodies' are out of touch with the rank and file of the neighborhood. This type of person is prone to overlook the great majority of people who have few rewarding contacts with social and cultural agencies, people with limited means whose potential interests have never been uncovered, who digress easily into the accessible and standardized forms of leisure time activities. These people, living far below their level of adequacy, often have vital needs: needs for advice in more efficient home management, counsel in the care of children, and guidance in the selection of better forms of recreation. But their needs are missed in the whirl of existing activities.

"Proof of this neglect and paradox is contained in some interesting investigations of the index of participation in community life. The procedure of these studies is relatively simple. From the membership file of all organizations in a town a composite list of names is compiled. This list is compared with the total number of adults in the community. In a certain 'over-organized' town, where 'every night in the week is taken,' only 34 per cent of the total adult population belonged to one or more organizations, while 66 per cent belonged to no organization. Of this 34 per cent, a great number belonged to only one organization, while a small number belonged to many. These specific figures may not apply to every community, but they probably represent a trend in community participation that is rarely understood by the active 'busybodies' who 'run' the town. In spite of the fairly respectable list of community enterprises and the apparent rush of card playing by afternoon and dancing by night, a realistic view of the whole community does not justify the smugness of the 'elect' nor does it obscure the neglect existing in the neighborhood." [2]

This, then, is America today. Two-thirds and more of the population of our towns and citizens are probably *engaged in nothing* of a public nature.

A first task we have to undertake is to make people aware of this fact—particularly those who are weary of much going out at nights to committee meetings, forums, and clubs. They need to be apprised of the fact that they and their kind are only a bare handful in the community, that they are the small group who do all the joining of good causes, most of the contributing, and practically all of the active thinking about public matters. These public-minded people need to know that the most pressing problem in our communities is to broaden the base of community participation. Many of them know this and are valiant in their efforts to achieve this broadening. But most of them, absorbed

[2] H. Y. McClusky, "Mobilizing the Community for Adult Education," *Michigan Alumnus Quarterly Review*, April 29, 1939.

in their special interests—of social settlement, or "Y.," or Boy Scouts—fail to see the wholeness of the community's problem.

Because of this, one of the most important projects now engaging the minds of public-spirited citizens is the establishment of community councils. Very few towns or cities have them. For the most part specific prosocial activities are carried on by groups of people who are in partial or entire ignorance of what other groups are doing. Frequently, too, groups are jealous of what other groups are doing. I remember the case of one church-forum director who was downright angry because a community forum was taking the edge off what he had been doing—even though the new forum was not draining the people away from his group. And we all know how churches look with pious suspicion at neighbor churches. There are communities in which Catholics refuse to join an interdenominational religious council. Over against this are instances in which Catholics, Jews, and Protestants work cordially together for the furtherance of community aims.

Our new neighborliness—through special, public-minded groups—must take on a new form of *e pluribus unum.* It must become a grouping of groups. Manyness of activity—even though it be good activity—is not enough. The manyness must somehow achieve unity of aim and direction. A community council should serve this function. It should exist not only to make prosocial groups aware of one another's existence, but also to further the means whereby they can co-operate with one another. In a previous chapter mention was made of a Catholic group of lawyers. When the group was described to a number of public-minded Protestants in that community, there was no knowledge of its existence.

Examples of our futile separateness of social activity and aim might be endlessly repeated. The pulverization of Americans into private-minded citizens is paralleled by their pulverization into public-minded groups. We need to find a way, in every community, of making our public-minded people aware of their community fellowship.

This is the first prerequisite to broadening the base of citizen participation. We need to begin the process of recovering and revitalizing our communities.

## IV

The early America of the town meeting has taken its place in history. But a new kind of America is emerging. At present it is only half-formed, for we are still largely an America of strangers. We may yet become an America of friends.

After all, the test of the quality of a people lies in

the breadth of their understanding and sympathy. Breadth of understanding and sympathy, however, cannot be created in a vacuum. To quote John Stuart Mill once more: "The whole people must participate; participation even in the smallest public function is useful."

These ways of participation are now open to us. The chief task of our newly forming democracy of neighbors must be to invite all its citizens to share in the work of building a nation of communities.

# 18

## WHAT A NATION CAN RIGHTLY BE

### I

Two of the oldest concepts that philosophers have discussed and rediscussed have been permanence and change. Sometimes the weight of their argument has leaned to one; sometimes to the other. But the conclusion of all their discussions comes to this—that both are necessary; neither is of any use without the other. Not much of a conclusion, perhaps; and hardly worth all the verbal to-do. But sometimes—particularly among philosophers—the fairly obvious truths take longest to get established in consciousness.

Perhaps this very simple conclusion is all we can say about what a nation can rightly be. It has, for its people, to be a source of permanence—of what they can safely bank on. It has to give them security and an assured orderliness of well-being. But it has also to be for them a source of change—of what they can expectantly look forward to. It has to give them the experience of an ever-fresh venturing into new futures.

Sometimes, when the life of its people is precarious, uncertain, subject to swift reverses, a nation places chief emphasis upon security. At other times, when their life moves along in even grooves, it places chief emphasis upon adventure. There is every reason today for our nation to be occupied chiefly with how to redeem the crazy and perilous haphazardness of its processes, to be concerned about how to bring security and fulfillment into lives where there has been too much of insecurity and unfulfillment.

Thus when we think today of what a nation can rightly be, it is not surprising that we think first of how it may remove its injustices, equalize its inequalities, bring life to the only partly alive. Inevitably today we think of the submerged, the unregarded, the unrespected. When we think in this way, freedom seems to us to have done not a little badly. Far too much, it has been freedom to make life unfree.

I have heard people say that all this prevalent seeking for security is craven. They tell us we have grown soft; that our forefathers were pioneers—tough ones—pushing on to new adventures; and that we ought to stop all this anxious talk about security and push on likewise. Brave words from those who have missed no meals, have lost no jobs!

We have to pause and take stock. Our nation has been hitting it up at a breathless pace. We have done so many things, we have not had time to estimate whether they were done well or ill. So we have run up our factories; thrown together our jerry-built cities; crowded our slums around the smokestacks; dug out the heart of our soil and the hearts of our people with tractors; bought up our politicians for the favors we have needed. For a number of decades now we have been hell-bent for prosperity. Some would say that this sentence should have ended without the last two words.

It has been a phase of our history. A phase of freedom—tough, adventurous freedom. An adolescent phase. Freedom with a minimum of considerateness.

Today we live in a world stunned by sorrow. The grief of millions hangs over us like a pall. Millions in our own land—shorn of self-respect; young ones and old ones, facing workless days, wondering about America, wondering about the land of the free. Millions in the rest of the world—waiting for the bombs to fall, fearing the kind of freedom that a dictator threatens to bring. We are brought up sharp. Freedom must be something different from what it has been—here and everywhere throughout the world. Freedom has to grow mature.

This is what we are learning and saying today. We

are not listening to the dictators. They are proposing freedom through force. To us this is only old enslavement. To us there is only one freedom worth while, the freedom of understanding and compassion.

This is the freedom our forefathers envisaged when they founded the nation. It is the freedom from which in large measure we have fallen away. Because we have fallen away from it, we have built our uncompassionate cities, have piled up our uncompassionate wealth, have visited our fellow men with uncompassionate defeats.

André Siegfried once wrote a book which he called *America Comes of Age.* To us, in our present disappointments and bewilderments, the title must seem to have been premature. America, we hope, is now in the beginning of the process of coming of age. For the sign of coming of age—of putting off childish and adolescent things, of becoming spiritually mature—is the deepening of the social sense. Immaturity is egocentric. Maturity is sociocentric. Maturity cares about people.

The hope that lies in us today is that we, as a people, may learn to care about people. We have had a breathless and adventurous time of it caring about things. That time has had its high points of excitement. Today, however, we are sobered into the realization that nothing counts if our people do not count. And we have been sobered into this further realization—that nothing counts if the people of all the world do not count.

## II

This is why we can no longer be concerned solely about ourselves and our own nation. A monstrous new philosophy is seeking to take possession of the world. It is the philosophy of force, of inequality, of war and conquest as the noble, heroic way of life.

The Italian dictator has expressed it thus: "Fascism . . . believes neither in the possibility nor the utility of perpetual peace. It thus repudiates the doctrine of pacifism—born of renunciation of struggle and an act of cowardice in the face of sacrifice. War alone brings to its highest tension all human energy, puts the stamp of nobility upon the people who have the courage to meet it. (Fascism) . . . is the education to combat." [1]

This is only saying in other words—words now made sanguine with the blood of countless innocent people—what Nietzsche said long ago: "For the present we know of no other means whereby the rough energy of the camp, the deep impersonal hatred, the cold-bloodedness of murder with a good conscience, the general ardor of the destruction of the enemy, the hollow earthquakelike convulsion of the soul, can as forcibly and certainly be communicated to enervated nations as is done by every great war. . . .

[1] Benito Mussolini, *The Political and Social Doctrine of Fascism* (London: The Hogarth Press).

"You shall love peace as a means to new wars—and the short peace more than the long. You I advise not to work, but to fight. You I advise not to peace, but to victory. Let your work be a fight, let your peace be a victory." [2]

Words like these give sinister meaning to the threat of Alfred Rosenberg, the official theorist of the Nazi party: "A new peace shall make Germany mistress of the globe, a peace not hanging on the palm-fronds of pacifist womenfolk, but established by the victorious sword of a master race that takes over the world in the service of a higher civilization." [3]

We would do ill to be deceived by the pretensions of "a higher civilization," of "a new world order." The new order envisaged is merely an old order—of master-slave, of command-obedience, of force-submission. They who seek to come to terms with this revived barbarism are themselves swiftly terminated. It brooks no rival. It cannot permit free minds and free enterprise. It must have only commanded minds and commanded enterprise. It vaunts itself as the freedom to end all freedoms.

We who care about democratic liberties must awaken

[2] Nietzsche, *Thus Spake Zarathustra.*

[3] Quoted in Frank Munk, *The Economics of Force* (New York: George W. Stewart), p. 24. This book should be read by every American. It tells of the far more sinister economic fight that the Nazis are out to wage against the democracies.

to this. Many of our businessmen, anxious about their foreign commitments, think they can do business with the dictators. "Why prolong the agony?" they anxiously ask. "After all, business is business, and these totalitarians will have to trade with us." It is a tragic illusion. These totalitarians are not businessmen. They are fanatics of a new religion: the religion of Power. They are the unrelenting opponents of Christianity and of the democracy which is Christianity's political and social expression. They, like Nietzsche, despise Christianity's doctrine of love and fellowship. Hate, for them, is the ennobler; division and conquest are for them the way of life. "The German race—that is our faith! It has higher rights than all others. . . . We have the divine right to rule, and we shall assure ourselves of that right." [4]

## III

Two tasks, then, confront us:—The first, and most pressing one, is to bend every energy we possess to oppose this rising power of barbarism. For if it wins in Europe, no matter how many miles separate us from that continent, we shall be the next object of its attack. Religious fanaticism knows no bounds. When, how-

[4] Dr. Robert Ley, chief of the government-controlled labor organization, in a speech delivered in conquered Poland. Quoted by Munk, *op. cit.*, p. 70.

ever, religious fanaticism is implemented by the most expert and diabolic techniques ever devised by man for disintegrating peoples from within, it becomes the most dangerous foe that freedom has ever faced.

But there is a second task, a longer and perhaps harder one: of achieving in our own land the generous freedom which is our reason for existing. We have, indeed, to hold on to what has been great in our way of life; but we have to bestir ourselves to attain an even greater way of life.

"Upon the maturity of our industrialism has descended a great terror. Force of purpose implemented by machines is different from any force ever unleashed before. It is impersonal and terrible. . . . It can be fought under democracy but only with a better purpose and a stronger will. That purpose cannot arise out of a passion for Sunday driving and 'every modern convenience.' That will cannot be conjured from our desire to blast Hitler, so he may leave us alone to golf and the movies.

"It can arise only from the resolution to raise up on this continent the ablest, hardiest and most intelligent men and women that ever inhabited the world. Only through that goal can our democracy survive." [5]

Our minds are the makers of the human world in

[5] Roy A. Helton, "Inner threat: Our own softness," *Harper's*, September 7, 1940. Condensed in *Reader's Digest*, October, 1940.

which we live. Only free minds can make a free world. In the past, our minds have been only partly free. In spite of our democratic faith, they have been bound by various ignorances, prejudices, class antagonisms, egoisms, fears. Hence they have built a world that, good as it is, is still only partly free. Our stronger faith must be in the achievement of minds that are fully free. Such minds will not be achieved easily. There will be needed the discipline of our aims and hopes, the learning of ways of drastic self-criticism. There will be needed the toughening of our will to understand, the awakening of our imagination, the vitalizing of our sympathies. There will be needed a new energy of action. These are the ways to freedom. They go before all political and economic arrangements, because they alone can create the arrangements that are good enough for man.

We Americans know that we have a job ahead of us. The dictators, by monstrous contrast, are setting for us the pattern of the job. Our free minds are to build a free world. This is what we are saying to ourselves today. And this we shall do.

We are turning the first page of a new chapter of history.

# INDEX